Glenn Martin (1950 -) grew up in Sydney, Australia. He lived in the hills on the far north coast of New South Wales for twenty years before coming back to Sydney. He has worked at many occupations: high school teacher, manager of community sector organisations, psychiatric nurse, community development worker and social researcher, as well as being a writer on management, employment law, training, and business ethics. He has been an editor of professional and academic publications, and is currently an instructional designer for online tertiary courses.

His previous books include:
   Human Values and Ethics in the Workplace
   The Little Book of Ethics
   The Ten Thousand Things: A story of the lived experience
     of the I Ching
   Sustenance
   The Big Story Falls Apart
   To the Bush and Back to Business
   Places in the Bush: A History of the Kyogle Shire

See Glenn's website at www.glennmartin.com.au

A Modest Quest

Glenn Martin

G.P. Martin Publishing

A Modest Quest
By Glenn Martin

Published 2017 by G.P. Martin Publishing
Websites: www.glennmartin.com.au
Contact: info@glennmartin.com.au

Copyright © Glenn Martin 2017
All rights reserved. No part of this publication may be reproduced or transmitted in any form or by any process without the prior written permission of the publisher, except for the inclusion of brief quotations for a review.
Glenn Martin asserts his moral rights as the author of this book.

National Library of Australia
Cataloguing-in-Publication entry
Author: Martin, Glenn.
Title: A Modest Quest / Glenn Martin.
ISBN: 978 0 9804045 9 3 (pbk.)
Subjects: Martin, Glenn.
Dewey Number:

Book layout and cover design by the author
Typeset in Bookman Old Style 11 pt
Printed by Lulu.com

Front cover: Mrs Nell Crowe, mother of Glenn Martin.
Family photo circa 1956: Glenn, Brian and Helen Martin, Valerie Brissett (cousin) and Sid Martin (father).

Author's Foreword

A Modest Quest describes the beginning of my quest to find out about my family. It was, at the outset, intended to be a modest quest – simply to find out about my parents' brothers and sisters and their parents. Growing up, I and my sister and brother thought that all our grandparents were already dead; nor did we know much about our uncles and aunts. But the quest has not been easy; it took about two years and some deep digging just to settle the questions about these relatives. By then, of course, the quest had embedded itself in my life, because you don't understand a person until you know something about their parents, and so it goes on.

The intention is that other books will follow, addressing particular generations or particular themes that are emerging. For example, a forthcoming book is called *They Went to Australia*. This looks in particular at the direct ancestors who came to Australia – all in the period from 1835 to 1860, and all from England, Scotland and Ireland, although let it also be said that Cornwall figures prominently.

The Arc of the Family

This is the title of the proposed series of books. It might require seven books to tell all of the story that I now know, and I am still digging, discovering and being surprised.

Glenn Martin
Sydney, December 2016

Contents

Author's Foreword i

Chapter 1: The beginning 1

Chapter 2: Rabbit holes and my parents' siblings 18

Chapter 3: Certificates, cemeteries and the discovery 39

Chapter 4: My mother's home breaks up 56

Chapter 5: My father's home breaks up 80

Chapter 6: The second horizon 93

Chapter 7: Where do occupations come from? 112

Chapter 8: Bethanga, Victoria 130

Family trees 155

Chapter 1: The beginning

The past becomes interesting and I become curious to know.

1

The family I grew up in was a pioneer family. It wasn't just that we lived in a temporary dwelling on a bush-covered block of land on a dirt road, with few other houses around. The family itself was a pioneer venture. There was (almost) just us. Neither of our parents had parents of their own alive. Both of them had a few sisters and brothers, vaguely – we had met some of them and knew their names, but mostly they did not have much to do with our lives. Beyond the occasional fact about our parents' parents, there was nothing.

Yet, there was, in all this, a spirit of hope. We were to be the children of opportunity. We would grow up with good schooling and learn an occupation – perhaps school teachers or nurses. Both mum and dad had had to leave school young. In dad's case, he was about thirteen when he had to leave school and get a job. In mum's case, she was about fourteen, although she went back later at night time and did Intermediate studies (which you normally finished at fifteen years of age in those days).

Essentially, we would achieve more than our parents had had the opportunity to do. There was something honourable in this, and we accepted the venture and looked to the future. Occasionally, as children, we would visit Aunty Frances and Aunty Pearl, mum's sisters. Mum had grown up with Aunty Frances from age twelve, so she was her closest family contact.

On dad's side, we knew Uncle Norm, because we had actually lived with him when we children were young. He and his wife were separated, and there was a daughter, Diane, a couple of years older than Helen, my big sister. Mum helped to look after her and the house. We moved to Greenacre when I was four. It was August 1954. I remember that I made an effort to memorise this date because it was an important date in my life.

We were on our own at Greenacre. It was silent and dark at night, and there was no one to call on. Nowadays you think of the telephone, television, instant contact any time. You assume you have a car, transport. No, we didn't – no car, no phone. No television until I was fourteen. There was a mantel radio that mum had on during the day when she did sewing. Occasionally I think she received letters from her sisters.

Down at the next intersection of the road there was a telephone box, about one hundred metres away. We went there if we had to ring someone, with four pennies. After a few years, in an emergency, there were now neighbours who had a phone, and we could go there and ask if we could use their phone. There was also a bus stop near the phone box, and we went to Bankstown or Strathfield (if we were going into the city) to go out. There was a butcher and a grocery store a few hundred yards the other way, from which mum ordered the weekly groceries.

We didn't have much money and we made do. The family was building for the future. And we did. We children, me and big sister Helen and younger brother

Brian, all grew up and finished school and yes, we became nurses and teachers. In all those years there was little contact with other family, and we figured that was the way of it. Modern life, living in a city that spread out to engulf us, looking towards membership in society as qualified, competent participants who earned money, started their own families and acquired their own houses with requisite mortgages.

We did have contact again with mum and dad's brothers and sisters. Dad died when I was sixteen. It was sudden, one Saturday afternoon when unusually, he and I were working together, replacing the roof on that temporary dwelling, which continued to stand, now at the back of the new house into which we moved in May 1959. We were on the roof, replacing sheets of rusty iron with new sheets (don't imagine for a moment that I was competent, I was just helping).

He got pains in the chest and had to come down. Mum was worried, and called the doctor. The Italians over the road had a telephone. The doctor came, and examined him. He advised rest, and said he shouldn't get back on the roof today. He should get someone else to finish the job. The doctor was just packing his bag to go when dad had the heart attack. The doctor sprang into action, hauling him onto the floor and starting to pump his chest. He summoned me to start mouth-to-mouth resuscitation, then he told mum to call for an ambulance. Someone went back over to the Italians' place. Dad's face was rough from not having shaved that morning. He didn't respond. The doctor said to keep at it until the ambulance arrived.

Mum went in the ambulance. I'm not sure what happened after that. Somehow I was at the hospital at eight o'clock that night with mum, and dad was lying on a table, dead, just completely still and cold, gone. I wasn't thinking much. All the thoughts had been pushed away. I knew I had a responsibility to be grown up and be a support to mum. She was shattered. I was empty, black.

Family arrived then. Mum's brother Victor came. He lived not far away at Bankstown, and his daughter was engaged to a policeman, who volunteered to go to a camp where my sister Helen was spending the weekend with a St John's Ambulance group. I don't know who was at the funeral. That was a blur, except for my seeing lots of my class mates from school, and the small church we went to being packed out into the street.

It was shocking to see my class mates. I was thinking, why are you here? I hadn't realised that death opens doors everywhere, and the most unexpected people walk in. You think your life is private, and suddenly it becomes quite clear that it is not. Everyone is there.

What was to happen to us? It was as if the roof of the house was still intact, still covering us, but all the walls had been blown out, and I couldn't understand why the roof was still standing up. This could have been a re-run of our parents' lives, with everything collapsing sometime in the teen years. But mum was resourceful and determined, and Aunty Frances turned up.

Mum is still alive at age ninety-two, and she still vividly remembers her sister Frances helping her then, sitting down and being practical, figuring out how mum could keep the family together and survive. She went with her to see the Department of Social Security, and worked out what support she could get with the Widows Pension, and how we children could stay at school and finish our education.

From such things I have some ideas about family. One aspect is this: it could be about people whom you may not see much, but you are in their mind and they will come around if you find yourself in need. Mum occasionally had her opinions about people in her family – sisters, brothers, her parents – so I knew she had some notions about family too. Life wasn't all about putting the past behind you and building the future.

2

Given the way we grew up, I had seldom given family much thought, in terms of parents' parents and so on. Mum had told us a few things; dad, very little. Mum had gone to live with Aunty Frances when she was twelve. I was given to understand that both her parents had died then, and the children who were still at home were split up among who would take them.

Dad's parents had also apparently died when he was young, and he ended up having to leave school early and go to work. He had an older brother, the Norm we lived with, and there were others about whom I had only vague notions. We knew there was another brother. In fact, amid the pall of the days after dad died, we received news that this brother had died the day after dad. He had had throat cancer. We knew dad had a sister, Thelma, because she had married Victor, mum's brother.

But it took until mum was ninety before I suddenly got interested. I realised that I could not name all of her siblings with any certainty, or dad's siblings. Over the years, I had asked mum a few times to name them for me, and I wrote them down on scraps of paper, but she wasn't even sure about all of her own siblings, and even less sure about dad's. I am just talking about names and the order of them; I am not even talking about dates.

One time while I was at mum's place, she showed me her marriage certificate. It had the names of both her parents and dad's parents on it, and I was surprised to see that dad's father had been a blacksmith. I had no reference points for this. Dad was a painter, but he had been introduced to that trade through mum's family, because dad had not had a trade when he married mum, and there were trade painters in her family. Her father had been a painter with his own business, but he had gone broke in the Depression. But dad learned how to be a painter, and he made his living at that until his premature death at age fifty-three.

I had no idea what being a blacksmith meant. Had he shod horses? And was that why dad had had no trade when he got married, because there was no call for horses to be shod anymore? It just reinforced that sense of being part of the relentless modern world and cut off from the past.

Mum's siblings went something like this: Tommy, Frances, Pearl, Victor, mum, Jackie.

Dad's siblings were: Norm, then the brother who died of throat cancer, Thelma (who married Victor, mum's brother), maybe another brother, dad, and I think there was a younger sister.

Mum's parents – Archer and Mackie. The Archers were English, the Mackies were from Scotland. They all came out here as free settlers; none of them were convicts. Whenever family history was mentioned, she always made this statement. It was as if it had quotation marks around it: "All of the Archers and Mackies who came to Australia came here as free settlers; none of them were convicts".

Dad's parents – dad's father's name was Martin, of course! I remember mum showing me a document which said that dad's family had been born in Victoria, another thing I had no reference points for. A few years ago she showed me her and dad's marriage certificate, and it said that dad's mother's name was Eggleston. Again, nothing I could relate that to. Given that we had always been told that all of our grandparents were dead, I should have noticed that there was one grandparent who was not described as 'deceased' on the marriage certificate: dad's father. But it was not until much later that I was to learn the truth about all of the grandparents.

So, I knew very little about my family, and that's how it had been for all my life until I got serious about finding out. I had some family "stories" that mum told me, like the "free settlers" story, which I had no reason to disbelieve. The Archers had owned a hotel down at Pyrmont in Sydney, near what is now Darling Harbour, so they had money and reputation. Mum's father was frowned upon by the Archers because he had "married beneath him" by marrying a Mackie.

The imprimatur for these stories was the fact that an aunty of mum's, called Aunty Dolly, had carried out investigations into her family's history. She had gone to England and Scotland and conducted what we now call primary research, looking at old registers and records. She had gone "a long way back". The jewel of all these stories was a love story. An Englishman, an Archer, had worked at the royal castle, presumably as a groom, and had met and fallen in love with a Mackie girl who was a servant there. They saved up their money, got married and migrated to Australia. They started up the pub at Pyrmont, the Duke of Edinburgh, naming it after the castle where they had worked.

It was a very coherent and heart-warming story. The only crumb of other information I had was that I was a fourth generation Australian. Now I know that even to say this, assuming that it holds some truth, has to be a simplification, because we have two parents, four grandparents, eight great grandparents and so on, and all of these people could have come out to Australia at various times.

After mum's ninetieth birthday party, and after my asking her again for what she remembered about brothers and sisters and where she grew up, I went home to start finding out, properly. I asked her if I could get a copy (with my camera) of dad's death certificate and her marriage certificate, and that was the beginning.

I understood her remembered experience of her childhood. It was coloured by the trauma of her parents' family breaking up when she was twelve. It was still not clear to me exactly what had happened then, but I understood the fear of losing home and security, and I felt now a deep appreciation of what she had shouldered and managed to achieve when dad died when I was sixteen. As a widow in her mid-forties with little income, she held house and home and her children together. But I wanted to know what the facts were, that she had wrapped her impressions around. It would help me to understand why it was that she remembered things the way she did. And beyond that, I finally wanted to know "where I came from".

3

Family, families. It wasn't long after I started on this quest that I realised that the word "family" covers a host of different realities with the same brush. When I say "family", do I mean all of it – everything that emanates from me backwards to the misted past? In fact, the only people whose "family" is exactly the same as yours are your siblings from the same two parents. Everyone else has a different family, including, most profoundly, your parents. Your dad's mother and father are completely different from your mum's mother and father. Your cousins have a lot of relatives in common with you, but there are a lot that are different too.

So what is a "family"? I decided that it is better characterised as a collection of families. It seems best to say that a family is a mum and dad and their children. So your parents are not just your family, they are part of another family too, the one they grew up in where they were the child with their own mum and dad. And of course, this is true even where the living facts are different. My mum had the family she was born into before she had to go and live with her big sister. My dad had the family he was born into before he had to go and live with his Aunt Maud and Uncle Paul. But I am getting ahead of myself.

If these are families, then the family tree I was about to fill in was more like a forest than a single tree. There are lots of trees, and looking backwards you can see they are kin; all these people are connected in some way by blood. But a new family, like the one my mum and dad made when they got together, is where kin encounters the stranger. The whole enterprise of family is a forest of trees, made up of kin and encounters, and it keeps growing through new encounters.

It was this idea of kin that puzzled me, the idea that I was connected with a host of people, most of whom I didn't know, or didn't know very well, by something deep, inherent, that we loosely call "blood". This was why I could meet one my cousins a few years ago at her mother's funeral (my mother's sister Pearl) and be transported back forty years. She looked just the same to me as when we were children, and that was the last time I had seen her, about forty years earlier.

It was why I could sit at the funeral for my mother's partner later in life, George, and see a man across the aisle and think, "I know that nose. That's the Archer nose." And it was my mother's younger brother, Jacky, who had been the little kid that had to get farmed out too when the family fell apart. He was about nine when my mother was twelve. Jacky hadn't been so lucky. He went to Tommy's place, and he got beaten up a lot and he left home in his teens and found his own way. He sounded like an Archer too when we talked – more like Pearl than my mum.

I didn't know Tommy's circumstances at the time, so I had few grounds for judging him. It was just more stuff that I didn't know – questions.

So, I had two certificates and a small pool of facts that were probably of varying degrees of truth or accuracy. I talked about my project to a few people. It was a modest project. "I just want to find out who my parents' siblings were, and their parents." Most people were sceptical that I would get far. They said things like "What are you going to do? Find out who the living are and go and knock on their doors? Good luck with that. They probably don't know anyway, or don't remember."

And, "If people are keeping secrets, they probably still want to keep them."

I said I was going to track down records. They said, "Sounds pretty dry. What's the point? Do you want to be one of those people who bore you with tales of aunties you never knew about and don't care to know about? Do you want to find someone famous? In any case, you're unlikely to find much. What's the point?" I said, "You've already said that."

I wasn't denying that they were right. I had lived for sixty years without knowing about family, and I made my own life anyway. The shape of my life wasn't dependent on knowing about my predecessors. I chose it myself, for better and for worse. I also appreciated the freedom I had had to do this. There are many people around who became a lawyer because their father was a lawyer and they were expected to become a lawyer so they became a lawyer but not a happy one.

Mum was always apologetic that she and dad couldn't give us any real guidance about what to become. I went to vocational guidance and they told me I could become anything. Doctor, engineer, surveyor, lawyer, accountant.... I had the brains, and they gave me brochures. That was a bit like a canary growing up in a small cage and suddenly being put out in the middle of a paddock and told to fly. Like that canary, I had no idea about flying. But at least I had a real choice, unlike that poor lawyer who was going to live all his life in a small cage. I was grateful to have the choice.

So I didn't need to know about the people of the past. I was pretty sure that they hadn't done any of the things I ended up doing. I went and lived in the bush; I knew they were all inner-city people (at least for a couple of generations). I went to university; they were all, as far as I could make out, were trades people, plus, I was told, some nurses and teachers. There wasn't anyone on either dad's or mum's side who had gone to university. So everything was new; leave the past behind.

But the recurrent experience of my quest has been surprise – "Oh! I didn't know that. I had no idea. Wow! What does that mean, in the great scheme of things?" It becomes different again, each time that I am surprised. The great scheme of things, for me, has changed. I have gone a long way past looking for my parents' siblings, and the great scheme of things is still changing.

4

I started with my parents. I hadn't searched the Registry of Births, Deaths and Marriages (BDM) before. That was a mystery, but as it happened, my eldest daughter's husband (Elvina's partner, Patrick) had recently qualified as a solicitor, and his first experience as a solicitor was at the Registry. He introduced me to its search engine, so I could get underway, try out theories and gradually, I hoped, narrow the field of search until the results were compelling.

I admit to dismay at the results of the first searches. You start off naively hoping that the findings will be obviously correct, and then they aren't. Either there is nothing, or there are many possibilities but none of them is clearly the right one.

He had a scout for my father's birth in the records, and said there were a few possibilities – one at Glen Innes, perhaps? Once I examined the certificates I got from mum, it was clear that the Glen Innes option was wrong, but it showed that you definitely needed quite a few points before it made any sense to try and join the dots.

However, I had to put a stake in the ground somewhere. I started with dad's birth, because I knew he was born on 5th December 1914, and for privacy reasons, the registry does not show births more recent than one hundred years ago. And I found it, because I knew from his marriage certificate with mum that his parents' first names were William Thomas and Elizabeth, and mum had told me he was born in Sydney, at Banksia.

But right at the beginning I was wrong. I had always assumed that dad was born in 1914, and the entry was telling me that he was born in 1913. What was going on? And this was all it was: I had calculated backwards from dad's age when I was a child, to work out his birth date, and I had never questioned it from then on. It was a simple case of me as a child doing a wrong calculation, and then there was never any reason for me or anyone else to question it.

However, what this experience did for me was to firm up my stance on the question of whether I would buy certificates. In the website, the entries give you some information, but not all. For births they tell you the person's name, the year, the place of birth and the parents' first names. They don't tell you the actual date of birth, and the more 'modern' birth certificates tell you who the other children were in the family as well. So I decided that, if I was going to be serious about this whole business, I was going to have to buy certificates.

I actually felt some excitement and nervousness about this at the start. It was a new area opening up in my understanding of my past, it was venturing behind a curtain and I wasn't sure if I was permitted. By mum? By the memory of my father? By other forces in the wider network of "family"?

And there were other voices too, the classic naysaying about digging into the past. When I mentioned family history to people, the spectres raised themselves up – genealogists don't have enough things to do with the rest of their lives; they bury themselves in the past so they can hide from the present; they are on a vanity quest to find someone important in their past so they can justify their own lives. Or, they are a writer or an artist, and they think there has to be some famous ancestor who was a writer or an artist, and that explains why they can write, or paint. They hunger for that kind of connection with the past.

I defended myself against these charges by keeping my venture modest – I just want to know the details of my parents' lives, and who their siblings were. I should at least know that, out of respect if nothing else.

Accordingly, dad's birth certificate arrived and there it was, in black and white – born on 5th December 1913. So here is how it would go. I would draw up a chart and it would have on it boxes for dad and mum, and their siblings, and it would state the vital details for each – birth date and location, and the same for marriage and death. It would have to include mum and dad's parents, of course.

Would the chart include the marriages and children of my parents' siblings? I should do that for the ones with whom we had had some connection, like the big sister mum went to live with. We had always been in touch with that aunt's children, our cousins. We knew who they had married and I could find out about their children. But apart from that, let's keep this modest and manageable. Stick to the "core" family.

There had to be some kind of template for Excel to make a family chart. I found one. It was neat, and it gave me plenty of room. It allowed you to put in siblings and it went back as far as great grandparents. I wouldn't need that, but it was good to have a roomy space that was well-constructed. All I had to do was find out the rest of the details.

I started by putting in myself and my brother and sister, then mum and dad, and I started putting in the names of mum and dad's siblings. Now I could see just what was missing, and what was unclear. Exactly how many siblings did mum and dad have? What were their names and ages?

Dad's birth certificate was already presenting questions. It showed that he was the third child. First there was Norman (yes, this is the uncle that we lived with until I was four), then there was William T. But no, there had been another: there was "1 male deceased", so dad had in fact been the fourth child. Well, I guessed it was no surprise that I hadn't known this; dad hadn't ever talked much and we hadn't asked too many questions. But he was still a sibling of my father's, so he had to be included. Something else to find out about.

And there it was again – the occupation of dad's father, William Thomas, was stated on the birth certificate, and it said he was a blacksmith. And he had been born in Victoria, at Bethanga. I could see how this investigation might make your head spin. From one certificate, I had a whole bunch of new questions. Where was Bethanga, what had dad's father done there, and how did he end up in Sydney? I even had the crazy thought – was dad called "Sydney" because his father had come up to Sydney to live? Dad's name was actually spelled that way, rather than the more common "Sidney".

I also had the name of dad's mother: Elizabeth Eaglestone, although I also picked up that her name was spelled differently on mum and dad's marriage certificate: Eggleston (where she was deceased). She was born in Balmain, and dad's parents were the same age, thirty. She had been born in Balmain, so William Thomas had presumably come to Sydney and met Elizabeth and they got married.

I was thinking about the claim that some people made, that if all you have is records and certificates, that makes for a very "thin" family history, dry and lifeless. But I could see story here already, and it was in the questions – what had William Thomas been doing in Bethanga, and why had he come to Sydney? I could see that I would get involved in social history, and the story would sit there in the space between the family records and the social landscape.

Why do I say this? Because I read my first piece of social history now. Let me say, gratitude for the internet and for tools such as Wikipedia. Whenever a new place or social fact has presented itself, I have been able to find out something about it online that put me into the social context of the time.

So, Bethanga. Where is it, and why is it? It is a little town in northern Victoria, not far from Albury in New South Wales. And when William Thomas Martin was there (prior to 1900), it was a mining town, gold-mining. Interesting. I parked that knowledge. Perhaps it would turn out to be relevant when I found out more.

To summarise, I had a small piece of the puzzle settled:

My father: Sydney James Martin, born 5th December 1913 at Banksia (Rockdale district in the NSW BDM). Died 4th March 1967 at Greenacre (heart attack, or "coronary occlusion; coronary sclerosis"). Sources: birth certificate and death certificate.

My mother: Alma Helen Archer, born 15 November 1923 in Sydney(?). Still living, January 2017. Source: personal communication from mother.

Yes, at some point I would have to formalise the facts about my mum.

Now, to attend to the marriage. Sydney James Martin married Alma Helen Archer in 1947 (personal communication). Then my sister was born in 1948, I was born in 1950, and my brother was born in 1952.

Mum said she and dad were married in a registry office, not a church. But they dressed up for it. Mum has a framed photo of them both, looking quite smart for those early post-war times when you had to know somebody just to be able buy new sheets for your bed. I'm not entirely sure of the reason for the registry office. Sometimes, even though I am listening to what mum says, the reasons get muffled.

Then I look at the marriage certificate again and I am troubled. It does not say they got married in a registry office. It states that they were married by the Reverend Herbert Begbie at St John's Church at Campsie (Church of England). Mum is 23, a dressmaker and a spinster. I look at the photo again (I have a copy). The photo shows them in a room; it could be anywhere, it doesn't mean they were married in a registry office. Was it just that she couldn't afford, or even obtain, a wedding gown, so in that respect it was just like getting married in a registry office, and that is what it has become in her memory?

I have to be content. I am not going to grill my mother for the "truth". I am interested that that is her experience of it this many years (more than sixty) later. She wore a very large corsage of flowers, and brown gloves that matched her brown bag. There was lace draped from the bag, and I remember her telling me recently that her mother could do beautiful crochet. Her mother had died years earlier, when mum was twelve – or so I still thought.

My father looks serious but also kind of peaceful. That's another story. He had been married before and his wife had died. There had been two children. But for now, to complete the record:

Marriage: Sydney James Martin and Alma Helen Archer, on 4th July 1947 at Campsie.

The witnesses to the marriage were Jean Gray and Victor, her older brother. There were no parents as witnesses. Three of the parents were marked as deceased; the only living one, dad's father, may or may not have been present. I don't know.

Boxes filled in on the Excel file. A start.

Chapter 2: Rabbit holes and my parents' siblings

5

My fear about this enterprise of writing about my family, or rather, my forest of families, is that I will disappear down rabbit holes and not be able to find my way out. But there have been different phases of this business, some of them quite clear in retrospect, and I can talk about them. Like the period of time where I visited cemeteries, found graves and read gravestones. Of course that happened a few times, but it was certainly a defined phase, because I waited until I had enough graves in a cemetery for it to seem worthwhile to pay a visit, and also because I ran into dry periods when I couldn't find out the next thing, so visiting a cemetery was a way forward, a hope that I would find something on a gravestone that I hadn't been able to find out any other way.

And yes, that happened. I found out things that were breakthroughs that I hadn't been able to get from records.

This first phase was circumscribed by the constraints on access to BDM records. I could only view and obtain birth records that were more than one hundred years old. For marriage records it was fifty years, and for deaths it was thirty years. This meant, for example, that I found my father's birth record, but I couldn't search for my mother's birth, as she was ten years younger. It also meant that I couldn't ascertain the birth my father's younger siblings, and this was a key part of my (modest) quest.

It took me a while to get into the swing of what I could find out and what I couldn't. Sometimes a death record will help you to identify the children of a person. For example, if I had the death record of my father's father, it would probably tell me who all of his children were, and their ages. That would be another way of finding out my father's siblings. I was keen about determining the siblings, both mum's and dad's, but some other things might have to come first.

The marriage certificate had details about my mum and dad's parents, and that was calling me, but there was also the matter of dad's previous marriage. This was no shock-horror surprise. This was part of known family history. Dad had been married before. His marriage certificate to mum stated that he was a widower. So here's that story.

Dad (Sid) married Olive Coates as a young man (I am filling in her name now; I never knew it before, but nor had I ever asked). He and Olive had two children – Jimmy and Pattie, but then Olive died. I can tell you now that she was only thirty-two, and she died of acute heart failure, soon after the birth of her daughter. Dad was thirty. This was 1943. As a man who worked for a living, what did he do about caring for his two young children, especially when one of them was a baby?

But Olive had a sister, Dorrie. Dorrie was married, but her and Wally couldn't have any children, and Dorrie wanted children. So dad went to their place to live, and Dorrie took over caring for the children. When dad met mum and they decided to get married, Dorrie thought she would lose the children, and she asked dad if the children could stay with her. And dad agreed to that.

I remember, as a child, going with mum to visit Wally and Dorrie at Lidcombe. They were Aunty Dorrie and Uncle

Wally to me. Maybe dad came too sometimes. There is so much you never notice as a child; you live in your own world. I don't remember much about Jimmy and Pattie. I do remember going to their weddings when I must have been around ten years old. My sister remembers dad crying at the church. There is so much I didn't know about my father. I don't think I ever knew what he felt. Sisters have different insights. They notice tears. I would probably have just run away, paralysed with fear.

There is a rabbit hole here, to do with Olive, but I'm not going there yet. I have a quest, a modest quest, and I won't even get that done if get led astray this early on. I have grandparents' names and their stories are not clear yet, but I am on the trail of siblings.

6

I think about what siblings I know from when I was growing up. Sometimes I used to ask both mum and dad how many siblings they had. The answers varied. Sometimes it was close to ten, on both sides, but when I pressed for names, it usually came back to the few we knew about.

This is what I started with for dad: Norm (older brother, we lived with him for a few years when I was young), maybe two other brothers – Billie may have been one of them, then there was dad, and then Thelma, a few years younger than dad (she was the one who married mum's brother, Victor) and then it got vague. Was there another child? In recent years when I asked mum, she seemed to turn "probably" into "definitely" and it was a girl, and maybe her name was Francie.

This is what I started with for mum, and it was a little bit clearer: Frances (the older sister she had gone to live with at age twelve), Tommy, Pearl, Victor, then mum, and Jackie. Moreover, this seemed to be the complete list, six of them, not ten, but I was never certain.

I am sure that some people find this state of affairs to be weird, and somehow reprehensible, on somebody's part. But I don't have their reference points. I have the reference points I grew up with, and it doesn't seem all that strange. From when we moved out of Norm Martin's house and went to live in Greenacre, we were on our own. We lived in a suburb that was still mostly bush, with a slow bus service to the nearest train station. All of these relatives lived closer to the city, in suburbs that were closely settled and had sealed roads.

We had no car and we had no phone. Television arrived in Sydney when I was six, but we did not get a television in our house until I was fourteen. I remember one night when I was maybe nine, our family got on a bus and went to Enfield (about half an hour), then walked for half a mile to the house of a friend of dad's, a man he worked with. The attraction was a small, black and white television in the lounge room. I suppose it was playing an American gangster-type show with fast cars and guns. We kids spent most of the night outside in the dark, playing. After that we walked the half mile back to the bus stop and waited for the bus again to get home.

We had a radio, a small mantel-piece model with a dark brown bakelite casing that mum and dad had saved up for, that dated from the 1930s. Mum had it on while she sewed during the day. We went to school and came home. Walking up the street was awful when it had rained, because the street was clay and it stuck to your shoes and it took ages to scrape off, and you had been at school all day and you were tired. Dad rode his bicycle to work for years, and he got home when it was near dark. Where was the room for visits to family members?

I think we were glad to get away from Norm's house too. I imagine that Norm was a nice man, and there was a lot of deep, mutual support happening in the housing arrangement, but sadness too, and I think both mum and dad were pleased to leave it behind. The arrangement came about because Norm was estranged from his wife, and there was a daughter, Diane, three years older than my sister, Helen. Norm seemed to have primary care of the daughter. Diane only went to see her mother on weekends.

Mum tells me that she used to pack the suitcase on Friday night, and then receive all the dirty clothes at the end of the weekend, so she could begin the cycle of washing again. She washed for our family – mum, dad and three kids, including nappies for my younger brother Brian – and for Norm and his daughter too. There was no washing machine, this was before the wonder of automatic washing; she had a copper to boil the water, tubs, a hand-ringer and a clothes line. Life was full; one was content if one had someone to depend on.

I haven't purchased every certificate that I could, so I don't have Norm's birth certificate. Maybe when I have exhausted my current lines of enquiry I will get around to that, but that may not be for some time, because I still have vexing questions, and they are testing my powers.

Nevertheless, I can tell you that Norman William Martin was born in 1909 at St Peters, as the first child of William Thomas and Elizabeth Martin, who were married in 1908, also at St Peters, which was William Thomas's domicile prior to his marriage.

This is Norm's story. He was a mill hand. Mum has told me that many Archers worked at Love's flour mills. It was a family thing. It wasn't just flour; they packed all sorts of food stuffs. Mum remembered her sister Pearl working there, and she got the worst job, packing pepper. When she went home at night her eyes were red and they streamed with tears. Everybody was looking for a way out, to find another job or position so they could leave the mill.

Given that this story was from mum, not dad, I see that I have another piece of the puzzle, because the question behind every new liaison or encounter in the family tree is, how did they meet? And for this generation, the answer in many cases is: at Clifford Love's mill.

Norm could have met his wife, Naomi, at the mill. She was a labeller. He was 31 and she was 23 when they got married at St David's Church of England at Arncliffe on 14th December 1940. It was five years before Diane was born. But their marriage didn't last. Naomi left him. She had met another fellow.

How do I know this? Well, because mum told me. But I now know more than this. I have viewed the records relating to his divorce, and I learned that the divorce occurred in two stages. In the first stage, he petitioned the court to decree a restoration of his conjugal rights. At this point, Naomi had left his house and was in a relationship with another man. Norm was looking after the child.

He also wrote to Naomi, asking her to come back home. My mum and dad are already living with Norm, and I am not even born yet. Norm says to Naomi, "As you know it looked as though I would have to put Diane in a home. Rather than do that I took what I consider the best course possible and brought Sid and Nell with their child here to live. They are going to look after Diane and get my meals and do my washing. Diane should be happy and peaceful here Bub, and you could come and see her a lot…I love you very much Bub won't you come home."

In the court documents, Naomi reveals that she is pregnant to the new man, one Jack Groves, and the child will be born just three months after me. She also writes to

Norm directly (three days before I was born, in May 1950), confessing her adultery in writing. She says, "I was going to tell you this for some time but couldn't work around to it." She tells him the date of the first act of adultery, in the park at Bronte, and that it has been happening once or twice a week ever since. "You can do what you like about it, Norm. All I want is peace of mind and Diane. Signed, Bub".

Why did she do it? Why did Naomi take up with another man? It doesn't seem as if she hated Norm, even given the law suits and insulting words. I have a couple of theories. Perhaps it was a case of defying the circumstances she found she had fallen predictably into. She worked in a mill, she met a man in the mill, she married him. And Norm was eight years her senior. I haven't proven it, but the searching I did suggests that Jack was much closer to her in age.

And then there was the excitement of a clandestine relationship, meeting and making love in parks. Mum told me that there was a parade of employees every morning in the mill. The manager was a devout but strict Christian, and there was a dress code – stockings for the ladies, and lipstick. It wasn't a place where you stepped out of line. Mum told me that they did manage to have fun there, but it all had to be below the radar.

In the second round of court proceedings, Norm withdraws his former suit and asks for dissolution of the marriage. In the meantime, there have been court hearings about maintenance, insulting words, and access. The divorce goes through in June 1950 (although the decree absolute dissolving the marriage was not granted until August 1951), and my parents continue to live with Norm for another four years. Sometime in 1954, Norm gets married again, to Frances Teresa Pryke. That is what must have triggered my parents to leave, and set up house in the temporary dwelling in the bush at Greenacre.

I know they had been trying for years to get their own place, but it wasn't easy. This is a story that I have been told a million times by mum.

Norm and Frances Teresa Pryke stayed married. I don't know if they had any children. He and the new wife later moved to the Central Coast, and when mum and George (the man my mum married about ten years after dad died) lived on the Central Coast they met up, and Norm and George became friends. So, when Norm died, his ashes were put to rest at Palmdale Cemetery near Gosford. Curiously, the ashes of mum's sister Pearl were also interred at Palmdale.

7

Getting to Greenacre

"It was hard after the war." That phrase flavours everything that mum has said to me about the period after the war. The remarkable thing, from the point of view of today, is that this statement does not refer to one or two years after the war; it refers to a span of almost ten years when life was tight, money was tight, and few worldly goods were available. You still needed coupons to buy many items, and housing was tight. When my parents first married, they boarded with a lady at Drummoyne, another inner suburb of Sydney. When mum and dad went to live with Norm, it was brokered by other brothers and sisters (I know mum's sister Frances was part of those discussions), who discussed the options for Norm and came up with the suggestion.

It was what you did – think creatively and collaboratively about where you could get a place to live, and sometimes family helped. This was a mutually beneficial arrangement. But mum and dad were determined to get their own place to live, to bring up their family. With what I have learned about where they and their parents' generation lived, I think their decision to go to the outer suburbs and buy a block of vacant land and build their own house was radical. All of the relatives for two to three generations had lived in the suburbs close to the city, suburbs that had been settled for decades. And none of them lived in a house they had built.

At the time they got married, Greenacre and Chullora were outer suburbs of Sydney, with dirt roads and scrappy bush cover, and the few houses that existed were spread far apart. Mum said where we lived at Greenacre had been a big chicken farm a few years earlier.

For four years they saved for a deposit on a block of land. I think it was 1953 when they looked at a new development at Yagoona, a few kilometres from Greenacre but similar, with blocks of land for sale. They met with the agent and selected a block of land and paid a holding deposit. A few weeks later they travelled from Wiley Park (Norm's place) to Yagoona to have a look at their dream block of land. I know this involved buses and trains and walking to get there, with two kids and a baby.

But it wasn't their name on the block of land, it was someone else's. They went immediately to see the agent, disconcerted. But the agent didn't miss a beat. He said, jovially, "Oh, don't worry. We can give you this other block further down the road," and he started to walk them down the road.

My father was a quiet man, but a couple of years before he had been in a fight with his employer, who had made him redundant and then had tried to cheat him out of nineteen years of long service leave. That case had gone to court with the support of the union, and he had won his dues. As I remember my father, he had a strongly imbued sense of justice. He was not about to be pushed down the street by a shady real estate agent.

So mum and dad refused the shady gent's offer, and he, of course, refused to give them their deposit back. It went to court, and they did get their deposit back, but it took months, and it also cost them, and they were back to the start. But the place at Greenacre came up and it was actually better, because it already had what was euphemistically called a "temporary dwelling" on it. There was a couple who lived there. They worked in a circus. They were packing up the last things in their little utility when we got there, close to dark sometime in August 1954.

That first night we slept on the floor, surrounded by boxes. We had fish and chips for dinner, wrapped up in newspaper, all sitting on the floor of that little building (I lie; it seemed huge to me, because it was all one room). I think mum and dad were bursting with joy. This was an unimaginably wonderful dream.

That temporary dwelling was our home for the next five years, until the new house did get built. The temporary dwelling was a one-room building with fibro walls and a corrugated iron roof on a concrete pad. It had small, louvre windows. I think it was probably built in the thirties. Maybe it was a worker's home when the area had been a chicken farm. It had a kitchen down one end with a tiny stove – even to my four-year-old self it seemed small, to cook for five people. The rest of the space was living and sleeping space. There was one divider – a curtain across the room. Mum and dad slept down that end of the room.

Off to one side of the building with an old wooden door was a room that had a bath in it and laundry tubs. Outside there was a copper with room for a fire underneath it, to boil water to wash the clothes. I remember there was jubilation when mum and dad managed to acquire an old wringer, which was fastened between the two tubs. I think one of the marvels of this place, from memory, was that there was a Hills Hoist clothes line in the yard, which stood like a harbinger of the future, as if we were destined for eventual greatness in our new abode.

Around us was mostly bush. There were a few houses here and there down the street, and lots of bush. This was my parents' great adventure, and as far I am aware, it was unprecedented in either of their families. They had no idea yet how they were going to be able to build a house, but they were determined to find a way. That determination, I knew at an unconscious level, was a response to the past.

Growing up I simply saw it as a social phenomenon, which is to say that this was post-war Sydney, and thousands upon thousands of people were doing a similar thing, figuring out how they were going to achieve the acquiring of their land and the building of their home. We were gradually surrounded by them in our street, and many of them had come from Europe. The Polish couple who moved in next door, for example, had been in a concentration camp in Poland and lost most of their relatives to Hitler's vicious lunacy.

All that was true, but now I also see what my parents were doing then as their own mission too, that had a lot to do with their own families. It seemed to me, even as a boy, that neither of my parents had had a settled childhood. They both ended up, not just having to leave school early, but their homes were broken up as well and they had to go and live with others. Now, in their humble first dwelling at Greenacre, they were going to build their own home and family. It was something they had not had themselves, but their children would have it.

8

Am I proceeding sequentially through dad's siblings? In any case, the next sibling was the male who died. His name was Albert, and he was born in 1910 and he died the same year. I haven't purchased the birth and death certificates, so I don't know how long he lived or the cause of death. I simply register this here as an experience in the life of dad's parents. Their second child died as a baby. I think of social history. Was this an unusual circumstance at the time, or was it common?

I learned that in 1910 in New South Wales the infant mortality rate was 70 per thousand, or seven per hundred. The infant mortality rate had started to decline, but seven per hundred makes it a reasonably common event. For comparison, the infant mortality rate now is less than one in a hundred. Who knows what sadness the death of Albert caused, or to what extent there was resignation about it?

The third child was also a male – William Thomas, named after his father. He was the next person to my father in the family, and was two years older than dad. I obtained his marriage certificate and it revealed that his occupation was "mill hand", the same as his older brother Norman. It is not too much of a stretch of the imagination to assume that he worked at the same mill as Norman, the one at Kent Street in Sydney. A similarly short stretch of the imagination would accept that the girl who became his wife also worked there. She was a typist, or "Typiste" in the marriage record, and in the 1930s the typist was an essential cog in the machinery of commerce.

I never knew anything about William. I assume he was called Bill. That was the era of short names and nicknames; at least it certainly was in the Martin family. Norman was Norm, Sydney was Sid, and so on. But there are two remarkable facts about Bill. The first was that the typist he married was named Holly, her full name being Holly Hammett Hook. She was a local girl, born in St Peters, and at the time of their marriage, Bill and Holly both lived in Arncliffe. The remarkable fact is that Holly is the name of one of my daughters, and I never had any idea that I had an Aunty Holly. I didn't choose my daughter's name, her mother did, and the name was chosen simply because she liked it.

The second remarkable fact is that Bill died just the day after my father. My father died on 4th March 1967, and Bill died the very next day. I mentioned him earlier. Still working as a mill hand, fifty-five years old, carcinoma of the larynx. Holly Martin lived on until 1996. I wonder what connection there was between my father and Bill. They were only two years apart; had they been close as children, playing the same games and getting up to the same larks? What continuing connection was there between them in adult life?

Dad had married his first wife in May 1935, and Bill and Holly got married a few months later, in January 1936. Bill and Holly stayed in the same area, around Arncliffe. Dad and Olive were at Leichhardt. Dad and Olive had their first child, James (Jimmy), in 1939; Bill and Holly had their first child, Phillipa (named after Bill Martin's grandmother), in 1940. Both couples had a second child – Bill and Holly had Barbara in 1942, and then dad and Olive had Patricia (Pattie) in 1943.

I suspect that there was a connection between these two families and it is not simply a random fact that the two brothers, dad and Bill, died a day apart. You don't have to make too much of this; it is just a matter of accepting that life throws up such resonances, and yes, they do indicate that there is, as you might say, water flowing underground. If there was a connection between dad and Bill, did something break that connection? We know the answer to that question. A tragedy. After the birth of Patricia, Olive died. (I mentioned this earlier).

Olive died suddenly, of acute heart failure. She was just thirty-two. I think baby Patricia was about two months old (as my mum told me, from what dad had told her). I have more to say about Olive later, but the pertinent fact now is that dad and his two young children went out to Lidcombe to live, with Olive's sister and her husband. And I suspect, by natural forces, there was little further contact between dad and his brother.

9

Now my list of dad's siblings looks like this:

Norman William Martin, born 1909, St Peters; died 24 December 1989, Riverwood. Married Naomi Leftley, 1940, Arncliffe; divorced, 1951; married Frances Teresa Pryke, 1954, Sydney.

Albert Martin, born 1910, Rockdale; died 1910, Rockdale.

William Thomas Martin, born 1911, Rockdale; died 5 March 1967, Kogarah. Married Holly Hammett Hook, 1936, Arncliffe.

Sydney James Martin (dad), born 5 December 1913, Banksia; died 4 March 1967, Greenacre. Married Olive Coates, 1935, Leichhardt; widowed, 1943; married Alma Helen Archer, 1947, Campsie.

This is followed by another brother, then Thelma, then another girl (we think).

Thelma is not so hard to determine. I had met her and Uncle Victor (my mum's brother) as a child, so I have a touch point of experience to relate to. I had also been to several weddings of cousins while I was growing up where I had been introduced to them and other aunties and uncles. I think this is the way of it in many families, that when we are growing up we attend occasions where there are uncles and aunts and other relatives whom we have only ever met at such occasions. We know little about each other and it doesn't matter. Life is full anyway. But you absorb without thinking about it that you are connected by blood with many people (kin) and with all the people they have entered into a family commitment with (encounters).

Although I knew approximately when Thelma was born – she was a few years younger than dad – her birth date did not come quickly. She was born after the hundred-year mark for the registry, so I couldn't search for her birth record there. Determining this date had to wait for several months, until I had established various approaches to searching. And was she still alive?

That question I did know the answer to. I asked mum. She gets a Christmas card from Victor every year (he is older than her, so he is well into his nineties), and a few years ago his Christmas message, usually of a perfunctory nature, included the news that Thelma had died during the year. But I didn't know which year that was.

The answers to these questions emerged after I started making contact with other family trees. Remember I had started posting the family information into an Excel spreadsheet? Well, the flow of information gradually filled up this small dam and spilled out. I needed something serious. I had no idea any more about how far this modest quest would take me. I needed a tool which would accommodate all the non-standard situations that would occur, and extend as far as I needed to go.

Already I had problems; my father had married twice, and there were children to both relationships. How was I supposed to store and display this kind of information? In the spreadsheet it was starting to get messy, and I hadn't even got to the grandparents. After looking at a few options, I ended up with a system that seemed to have the facility to accommodate multiple, complicated connections. It allowed me to store the information on my computer rather than somewhere else on the internet in a space that someone else owned.

The system I chose also synchronised with a web-based tree, so I could invite people to look at the growing family tree online, and in addition it allowed me to look at other trees, and allow them to see mine. It was in this way that I found another tree that had details about Thelma, and it seemed to be on the mark. The person who hosted the tree seemed to be about four or five steps removed from me, so that was interesting – my first peep into a world of people on a similar quest and who were connected with me, near or far.

In a similar way I found out the date of Thelma's marriage to Victor. I was able to cross-check this against the record in the BDM registry, which validated the year and place. Accordingly I can state the vital statistics of Thelma's life.

Thelma Ellen May Martin, born 5 September 1918, Sydney; died 25 July 2009, Auburn. Married Victor William Archer, 12 July 1941, Canterbury.

Now for dad's other brother. I didn't know his name yet, but I did know a story about him. I don't know when I first knew this story. I remember mum talking about it with us children when I was in my late teens. Maybe it came up after dad died. Maybe I knew about it when it happened, but I have no memory of that now. My sister remembered; she told me this recently.

She said she was about ten (so I would have been eight). News arrived that dad's brother had killed himself. She thought that he had shot himself. Dad had to go and identify the body. He came home with a suitcase of his clothes, which mum sorted through for a charity. Dad was very quiet. I asked mum (this is in my late teens) if she knew why dad's brother killed himself.

She said he had been engaged to a girl, and she had broken off the engagement. He was broken-hearted. She said it was messy sorting out his affairs, because he had owned a block of land in the (Blue) Mountains. The rates hadn't been paid on it for several years, so there was money owing to the council. In the end, the block of land was sold off and the money all went to the council.

Okay, well at least that is a story. It has internal coherence. I guess a family is a bit like a world tapestry, and it probably contains a sample of everything you find in the big wide world. Now we had a sad story about a romance and a suicide. I wanted to touch the facts now, and see what I could verify.

Finding the birth was difficult to ascertain, because it occurred after 1914. For a while I thought that his name was William George Martin and I managed to construct a whole life story for him. He was born about 1915 and married Hazel Coggins at Rockdale in 1946. He died in 1973. His father was called William and his mother was Elizabeth, which fitted with what I knew from dad's marriage certificate. It was all persuasive so far. But then I looked at the burial details at Woronora Cemetery (yes, I had discovered the cemetery's search facility). This William George was Roman Catholic, so, no, it was definitely not him.

The Martin family seemed to be Methodist and/or Church of England. I couldn't accept that this brother was Catholic, and I also realised that along the way I had married William off, and we know that that didn't happen.

I didn't resolve this issue until I had obtained dad's father's death certificate, which was another long quest. When I got it, it listed the names of all his children, and among them was "George E. 40". This death certificate also confirmed William Thomas Martin's name, and his wife, Elizabeth. And that enabled me to search for George's death. I started in 1958, because my sister said she was ten, and I thought she must have been pretty clear about what age she was when the death happened.

I did find him, but it was in 1961, not 1958. I was starting to appreciate how our memories massage the past. My sister was actually thirteen, not ten. What was more incredible to me was that I have no memory at all of this happening. I was eleven; was I really that oblivious to what was happening around me? Apparently. I spent a lot of time reading books. I would go to the library and borrow six books (because the library said I could). I would have to hide a couple under my bed, because mum would say, "That's too many books. You have to get outside too, and play."

That sounds like sensible advice now, and I should probably still take it. I was very serious then. I was diving in deep, to find out everything, to experience other peoples' lives, and books gave me that. As it turns out, I missed some real things. It's funny: the shock of this realisation happened when I looked at the registry record of George's death and did the arithmetic on the years, to find out I was eleven at the time, and the event had passed me by.

I have to note here that there was, in the record, a minor niggle. George's father was noted as William Thomas, which is what I understood it to be, but his mother was recorded as Elizabeth May. The second name was the niggle. I had not seen "May" before and I wondered whether I had a problem. Would all my carefully gathered and sifted facts yet prove to be a house of cards that would collapse again into chaos?

Later, I would establish that Elizabeth's middle name was Hannah; it was on her birth certificate, and thereafter on records she was either just Elizabeth or she was Elizabeth Hannah. I was learning that when you looked at records, everything they said was not necessarily true. You had to try and figure out which facts you could depend on. Which facts were really true, which facts were mistakes, and if so, what was the nature of the mistake, and which facts were attempts to rewrite history – and if so, what was the reason?

I don't have an explanation for "May". The first question about it would have to be, who was the informant on the death certificate? It was Norman, George's older brother. So now I am interested in how the mother's name is given on the death certificates of all the children of William Thomas and Elizabeth Martin. I only have the death certificates for dad, William Thomas and George. I look at the certificates and I write down what I have:

- George's death, 1961; informant is Norman (brother); mother's name is Elizabeth May Eggleston (her maiden name).
- Dad's death, 1967; informant is Alma H. Martin (wife); mother's name is Elizabeth Eggleston.
- William Thomas's death, 1967; informant is Holly Martin (wife); mother's name is Eglestone. Christian name unknown.

I find a disturbing uncertainty about all this. I go back and look at dad's two marriage certificates. With his marriage to Olive Coates (1935), his mother is named as "Elizabeth Egleston (deceased)". With his marriage to mum (1947), she is named as "Elizabeth Eggleston (deceased)". A minor point? Perhaps, but I am getting the feeling that they didn't know for sure. And why is that?

I know what people might say. They might say that people weren't that fussy about spelling until recently, and that people didn't have the schooling that we have now, so they made mistakes. But those are general statements. I am interested in this particular family, and in this particular instance of variable spelling. I sensed that there was something wrong about it that was not to be explained away by these general truths.

But I can say this for sure about George:

George Edwin Martin, born 1915, Sydney; died 12 August 1961 at Sydney Hospital; usual residence, Ashfield. Unmarried.

Further, I can say that he died of a fractured skull and injury to the brain, and that there was an inquest into his death. More than that I do not know, and memories are unclear. In other conversations I have had with mum and my sister, the possibilities were that he jumped off a height (a bridge?) into a canal and drowned (the death certificate would appear to discount that theory) and that he jumped off a building (more possible). There doesn't seem to be any gun involved. The only evidence I have found of a gun in all my family history searching is one person who was a soldier during the Second World War, not a blood relative but the spouse of a blood relative, and even then there is doubt: he was in the army but he was a lorry driver.

[Further note about George: As I was finalising this book I had contact from a person on dad's side of the family, someone I did not know of, Nola Nixon. We are second cousins – our great grandparents (Thomas and Philippa

Martin) are our common ancestors. She had a slightly different version of the circumstances of George's death.

In her version, the lady to whom he was engaged died, rather than rejecting him. And he had died by jumping off the Observatory Tower in Sydney. So, yes, he died by jumping off a building, but less certainty about the end of the relationship with the lady.

Nola also said that Georgie used to come to visit Nanna Martin as drunk as a skunk and would yell out "Here I come. Are you home, Mrs Martin?" and all the kids would laugh, as you could hear him coming for miles. (Nanna Martin would have been the surviving wife of Georgie's father's brother, Norm; this Norm had died in 1933.)]

Chapter 3: Certificates, cemeteries and the discovery

10

It was difficult to find the last child of William Thomas and Elizabeth Martin. I was guessing that it was a girl; that was what mum seemed to suggest. But it was a long way round to get to her. I figured that the rule was this: if you can't find a person, fill in the space around them, and maybe they will pop out of that space.

What I had to do was focus on the parents. If my modest quest was to identify my parents' siblings, it seemed that I would have to push a little further in order to do that. I was familiar now with the BDM search process, and how to buy certificates. I started to add up how much I might have to spend on this quest. At around $30 per certificate, and if I bought a birth, death and marriage certificate for every person I found, this could be an expensive project.

I decided to concentrate on direct ancestors first, and not expand too far sideways. My parents' siblings would lead to marriages, and their children, and their children's marriages and their children as well, but I was interested in direct ancestors, not in having the biggest family tree in the world. "Scope creep" is always lurking. And yes, it would cost money, but it would be relatively small and intermittent, not a huge one-off cost.

The internet had brought the research within reach for me. There was an aunty of my mother (I was never quite sure what "aunty" meant; every adult older than us who had a family connection, no matter how remote, was called Aunty or Uncle) who did research into family. She went to England

and Scotland and searched out primary records. Mum said it cost her thousands of dollars.

Mentioning the aunty raises another issue: names. This aunty was Aunty Dolly. I guessed that this wasn't her "real" name in the birth records or at her christening, but what was her real name? Mum didn't know. She had always been Aunty Dolly. The same could be said of my mother. She is Nell, not Alma Helen, and she says she was called Nell from when she was a little girl. Anyone looking for her in the records would have to know that.

The only way I found Aunty Dolly was because I found her in someone else's tree and it had Dolly in brackets next to her real name, which was Alice Lilian. The other wonderful thing about this discovery was that I figured that the information in this tree was what Aunty Dolly had gone to Britain and discovered. It had migrated online and was there for sharing. Very cool. Which is why I have kept my tree open, because if I have the benefit of other people sharing, I should do the same.

I haven't got to mum's siblings yet, but the name issue came up there several times. Her older sister, Frances, as it turns out, was not christened Frances. She was Alice Frances, and actually a niece of Aunty Dolly, another Alice who was not called Alice. I told mum about this, but she didn't know about it, so it was confusing to her. But she did tell me that Noelene, Frances's youngest daughter and my cousin, was not christened Noelene. She was christened Noreen.

The problem was that when she was grown up and wanted to get a passport, she couldn't get one in the name of Noelene. To get one she had to go to her local Member of Parliament and get him to make representations for her. My name is Glenn, same as on my birth certificate. Not many people get confused about that.

11

I had purchased birth certificates. If you have an idea about the person's name, the place and the date, mostly it narrows down to only a few options, or ideally, just one. But marriage certificates are bit trickier. You have the bride and groom's names to work with, and the year and the place of marriage. This is what you get when you carry out a search. This is not always enough. Sometimes you want to have the bride and groom's parents' names as well, but you don't get that.

I was looking for dad's parents' marriage. It was a stake in the ground I needed. Would it be easy to find? It had to be around 1910. I took a date range of 1905 to 1910, and there were twenty-five persons by the name of William Martin who got married in that period. (All of this searching so far is confined to New South Wales. I am at this point ignorant about searches in other jurisdictions.) Suppose that I only know Elizabeth's first name. Then I would have two choices in the date range – Box (1908) and Eaglestone (1909). They are even close geographically – Redfern and St Peters.

But we know from dad's marriage certificates that the correct record is the Eaglestone one (aside from the spelling on dad's marriage certificates). The record tells us that at that time, her name was spelled "Eaglestone". I obtain the marriage certificate and it gives me new facts to work with. Later on I look for Elizabeth's birth certificate and it is spelled the same too. So I shift to thinking that the uncertainty about the spelling for her name came later on, as if she was at a distance, and there was no one to ask, or confirm, how her name was spelt.

At the moment I am interested in the last child of the marriage. The marriage certificate just puts the facts of William Thomas and Elizabeth's marriage in place. Now I will have to find the death certificates for both of them. That will list all the children and their ages. I go back to the death certificates and other marriage certificates I have for dad and some of his siblings, because I need to have some idea of when the parents died.

Dad's first marriage certificate (1935) tells me that his father was still alive then and his mother was dead. The William Thomas and Holly Martin marriage in 1936 raises some doubt; none of the bride and groom's parents are said to be deceased. But maybe the minister (Methodist) just didn't see the need to record this. Similarly in 1940, Norman William and Naomi's marriage has Norman's parents (Elizabeth is spelled Eaglestone) but no one is described as deceased. And dad's second marriage (in 1947) recorded Elizabeth again as deceased.

I can't get to the last child until I find out about her parents' deaths. It seems that dad's father was still alive in 1947, but I have possibly conflicting records about dad's mother. She may have died as early as before 1935, and the marriage certificates of her children simply didn't mention this. Or, some of this information is wrong, and which information, and why? I also note who the witnesses are at the marriages. Do the parents show up at any of them?

At dad's first marriage, both of the witnesses are from Olive's side of the family – her mother, and her brother-in-law. At William Thomas and Holly's wedding, the Martin witness is Norman. At Norman's own marriage there is no Martin witness, unless you count Victor, as a brother-in-law. This is all I have; there are other marriages, but the pattern is that I am not finding the parents at the marriages of their children.

This problem sits for some weeks. I fill in other spaces in the tree. I have found quite a lot on mum's side. Then I decide it is time for a tour of a cemetery. That has to be an essential part of a family history project. I have been compiling burial and cremation details from the death certificates I have been obtaining. There are many that are at Woronora Cemetery near Sutherland, for both mum's side and dad's side. I prepare a list and contact the cemetery to get the location of the graves.

12

I have been sharing this story with my children as I go. They all know who their parents' siblings are, and their grandparents. My goodness – I am a grandparent. My children are amused and at least tolerant of my ruminations about the project, and interested in my discoveries. After all, it's got to be interesting to learn now that their great grandfather was a blacksmith. What is that about? What is the context? Given that my father was a painter, you would ordinarily guess that the past contained more of the same – more painters.

The irony is that it was my mother's side of the family that introduced dad to painting. When he married Olive, his first wife, he was a storeman. It is mum's father whose occupation, on his death certificate, is "painter".

When I told my youngest son, Rohan, that I was going to go on an expedition to the cemetery, he was interested. I think he liked the idea of wandering around a cemetery with a purpose, and looking for graves.

I had been there before, a very long time ago. I remember accompanying my mother when I was young, perhaps four, on a day trip to Woronora. I suppose my sister was at school, and Brian, aged two, was being looked after by someone. This makes me think it was an event of some significance to mum. Is it surprising that I remember this? Not to me. There are huge expanses of childhood experience that I don't remember anything of, except in a process sense. I know I went to school every day, I know we went to the beach many weekends during summer, but particular events, not so much.

But there are a few things that got stored in my memory from the first few years. Mostly they are fragments. I remember the choko vine growing behind the garage at Uncle Norm's place at Wiley Park, and all the chokoes, but that is probably because I hated eating chokoes. I remember the milkman delivering milk one day, early in the morning. He had a horse and cart in the street, and he ran onto the verandah to fill up our billy and put the cover back on. When he called to the horse, it moved a few steps further up the street.

So I remember the cemetery. It was a sunny day, and mum visited two double graves. She stayed a while at each to pull out weeds and tidy up. She came prepared to do that. And when she had finished, each time, she sat there for a while. She told me that at the first grave were her parents, and the second grave was their parents. I was tired in the afternoon because we had to walk all the way back to Sutherland Station, and then there were two trains and a bus to get home.

This is what I think it was about. I think it was just after we moved to Greenacre, and I think the visit, for my mother, was about joy and sadness. She had been married seven years, and all that time, her and dad had lived with other people, because that was how they survived, and that was all that was available in those years after the war. Now they had three children and they were in a home, humble as it was, of their own, and would one day build their own new home. It was momentous, and as far as I know, building your own home was unprecedented in the family (meaning the family of mum and dad's siblings).

Mingled with that was the sadness, that both her parents were dead and they never got to see any of this, and mum never got to share her joy with them. It was a visit to say, "Hey, I want to share this with you, my gladness, after all the sorrows of my childhood, with you both dying and the family breaking up. I am sorry you aren't here now, but I also want to tell you, 'I am okay. Life is good.'"

Her father had died at 49 years, her mother at 52 years. It led to one of the great family myths of my mother's, that "people in our family die before they reach fifty". I know you may quibble about the arithmetic here, but there is a reason for that. Later. I remember as my mother approached fifty that she was seriously anxious about it. She really feared dying before she turned fifty. And when her birthday came and went, I noticed the relief in her, as if she had been given a reprieve. There was a huge event behind this, I knew that much. That stuff is strong. I remember as I approached fifty that I had to remind myself, "This is silly." And my dad had died at fifty-three; that didn't help.

Aunty Frances, her big sister, got breast cancer in the year before she turned fifty, and it looked as if she might die true to the myth. But she recovered, and lived many more years before she died. She lived to be sixty-four. So, one of my missions with the family history was to test the truth of some of these myths.

I figured that the other grave mum and I had visited was the Mackies, her mother's parents, for two reasons. The first was that mum related to the Mackies. They had come from Scotland, and she seemed to be proud that she had some Scottish blood. The second reason was that mum felt estranged from the Archer family. Why? Because the Archer family thought mum's father had married beneath him. It would make very strong sense to me if that second grave had been a Mackie grave.

Would any of this make sense now, so many years later, and armed with names and dates and grave locations? Or would it be disappointing and fractured, with nothing fitting in with the story?

Rohan is a person who likes to slow things down. We drove across to the other side of Sydney on a Saturday morning and found the cemetery and parked the car, and the cemetery was one way and a short walk in the other direction was a café. He voted for coffee first. I had sheets of paper with lists of names and gravesite references, but he thought it would be nice to enjoy a cup of coffee before we got into that.

It was February, and again it was a sunny day. The café was in a quiet street, even though it just a few steps from the station. There was, appropriately, a florist shop nearby. The café was a strange but welcoming place, as if some hippies from the seventies had been forgotten about and allowed to continue on, as if modern business imperatives had not encroached upon them to steal their soul. It had a splendid array of breads and cakes as well as lunch dishes and the smell of coffee. The front of the shop opened up completely, with shutters that opened onto the street outside, and there were chairs and tables on the footpath.

We had coffee and cake, while I went through my list and plotted a search plan. I had locations for Thomas and Margaret Archer (mum's parents), George Briggs and Frances Emily Mackie (Margaret's parents), William Thomas Martin (dad's dad, but not his wife), Edwin and Ellen Eaglestone (dad's mother's parents), and another generation back in dad's family, Thomas and Phillipa Martin (dad's grandparents).

It was fabulous. We found everyone on the list. Finding graves is not easy. You are given a section, which could contain hundreds of graves, and a number.

The numbers are supposed to be logical and sequential. The problem is, on most of the graves, the identifying number wore off many years ago in the weather. You might have to walk down a row and examine twenty graves just to find one number. Then you might have to walk for another twenty graves to find another number. Then, from the two numbers, you have to figure out what the sequence is. And you have to do this for the next row as well.

Nevertheless, we found our quarry, and I did it in the order that I wanted. I wanted to see mum's parents first, then the Mackies, then the Eaglestones and the Martins. I did not find it difficult at all to imagine the small boy I was when I did this about sixty years ago. Everything fitted, even the slope of the land and the gum trees, and the wide asphalt road up to the crematorium in the distance at the top of a rise. Thomas and Margaret Archer were resting, their names as bright on the smooth speckled marble as they must have been when they were etched over seventy years ago.

George Briggs Mackie and his wife Frances Emily presided over a more formal headstone fashioned from white marble in the likeness of an open book with a rope and tassle for a bookmark. Stained with the weather of many decades. But I did note that while George had died when mum was three, Frances died when my mum was eleven, so perhaps she knew at least one of her grandparents.

The Eaglestone gravestone (my father's grandparents) was more weather-worn because it was carved out of sandstone, but of a more stately shape, as appropriate for a man who was a stonemason. It was late morning and the sun was at an angle that probably made it the best we would get to be able to read the writing. I took lots of photos at different angles and took them home and played with the light on the computer in Photoshop to try and decipher the messages.

Rohan and I lay down on the ground to look at the writing from different angles and I wrote down the words we could work out. Eventually, between what we did on the day, and what I figured out on the computer screen, I got all the words: "In loving memory of my dear husband Edwin, died 7th January 1916, aged 58 years. May he rest in peace. Erected by his loving wife. Also, Ellen Elizabeth, wife of the above. Died 6th June 1937, aged 78 years."

We went back to the café for lunch. This time there were more people, mostly young, casual, probably mostly local, at various stages of a meal. What was the surprise, however, was the girl sitting on the footpath in the outdoor part of the café, singing. She was in her early twenties and had a nice voice and sang lovely songs, and Rohan and I had a beautiful lunch and it was all kind of perfect for a day at a cemetery discovering your ancestors.

After lunch we walked back to the cemetery, a bit further this time, to look for dad's side of the family. We were looking for a double grave where William Thomas Martin would be, with his parents, Thomas and Phillipa, nearby. My deeper interest was in finding an explanation for Elizabeth Martin.

The structure of graves, I think, tells you a lot about the dynamics of a family. What Rohan and I had seen so far this day was straightforward – two double graves with husband and wife in each. It was not so simple when we got to the Martin grave. Yes, we found William Thomas, and Thomas and Phillipa, but the configuration was interesting. The grave was presided over by Thomas and Phillipa Martin. I thought: grand, spacious, but a family still connected with the earth, not deeming themselves to be above it. Phillipa had died at 72; Thomas had lived to 89. But the grave also contained William Thomas, their son, and my father's father. He was appended below, and I thought: this is a man who had been married and who had seven children. I would have thought that he would have a grave of his own. And where is Elizabeth?

In addition, there was another person in the grave, another son of Thomas and Phillipa: Norman. I didn't know about him, and what was his story? Why is he here as well?

Looking at the grave, I thought, I knew nothing about my father's family until I started searching, and I have found my father's father, but now it looks as if I need to know more about my father's grandparents. They seem to have been quite sure of their place in the world. The other thing about this stage of my quest was that Thomas and Phillipa had not been born in New South Wales; they had come up from Victoria. It looked as if I was going to have to spread my wings to Victoria if I was going to find the answer to the questions that they presented. And I still had not found William Thomas and Elizabeth Martin's youngest child.

13

It was the single word on William Thomas Martin's death certificate that bored into me: "Married". The death certificate was saying that, when he died in 1955, William Thomas was married. If that were the case, it meant that Elizabeth was still alive in 1955. But how could that be? As early as 1935 she was described, on dad's marriage certificate with his first wife, as deceased. How could someone who was alive be described as deceased?

Apart from the records, which clearly were not being helpful, the only source of information I had was mum. The family trees had not contributed much about dad's family. Obviously no one had been interested in dad's family (yes, I know, the word "family" is used in so many different senses) until I came along scratching at the surface. But I knew there was something disturbing underneath the surface, and mum was really uncomfortable talking about anything to do with dad's family. Sometimes I thought this was simply embarrassment about not knowing, and I have plenty of sympathy for that embarrassment, given how oblivious I was about things that were going on when I was growing up.

But of course there was something more to it than that. I have skirted around this for years with mum, just approaching it from different directions. I managed to piece together something of a story after numerous forays. There had been another child born after Thelma, a girl, and the mother then had had some kind of breakdown. She had been taken into an institution. After I started doing the family history in a deliberate way, I told mum, watching carefully to see if this would set off alarm bells. I tried to pitch it as an unthreatening enterprise. I simply wanted to know who mum and dad's siblings were; I was curious, as children can be, even if they over sixty.

She would say, "I don't know much about your father's family." Gradually, over several visits, I got to saying, "I have managed to identify all of your siblings, and almost all of dad's. There is just this gap about this youngest child. I know there is one, and she was a girl, born about 1920, and the mother had a breakdown, but where did she go?" I wasn't going to raise the issue of when the mother died. I would get there somehow myself. I just wanted a clue as to where to start.

And there was a time, one occasion, when mum told me some important things. "I think her name was Francie. After she was born, her mother started acting strangely, and wasn't looking after her properly. She would do things like giving the baby a bath, but not thinking about whether the water was too hot. She was admitted to a mental institution. I don't know what happened after that. Your father was brought up by his Aunty Maud."

This was significant, and unprecedented, so I was brave, and I asked the next question: "Do you know what institution she was admitted to?" and mum said, "I think it was Callan Park." And then we talked about something else. It was enough. Also, I am getting better at the arithmetic of people, and I am acutely aware that what she has told me is based on what dad told her, and he was a child of seven at the time. I can't imagine how scared I would have been at age seven as one of six kids, with a father who worked a full-time job in an engineering workshop and a mother who was losing touch with reality while she was having to keep a household together and look after a baby.

When mum says the name of institution, the enormity of the situation starts to sink in for me. When I was a young adult, Callan Park was still going strong as a mental institution in Sydney, with hundreds of patients. It had been going since the 1880s, so it was a sandstone institution. It had lock-up wards and a reputation for toughness.

Let me tell you what reference points I have for this. After I left school, in the late sixties, I went to university, but I didn't finish a degree, and I ended up teaching. I didn't really want to be a teacher, and after three years I left. At that time, several people whom I knew from school had gone into psychiatric nursing. Why? Here is my best explanation: The Beatles had come along in 1964 and blew open all the doors that had been locked since long before we were born. Then in 1968, students around the world revolted. So everything was up for questioning, everything had to be looked at again, and we needed to know the truth about how things were.

Being a psychiatric nurse was part of the mission, to find out about how society treated people who were not "normal". I had to do something after leaving teaching, and psychiatric nursing struck me as being a critical element in understanding how our society worked. So I did it: I applied to Parramatta Psychiatric Centre to work, and I got a job there. It too was a sandstone institution; it looked much like the gaol down the road. It had a reputation of being tough, but Callan Park was said to be tougher. So you ask, what do you mean by tough: does it mean that the patients were tougher, or the ruling regime was tougher? I suspected that the truth was the latter.

Now here's the kicker. I may have worked at Parramatta, and mum may have been acutely uncomfortable about my choice, without being able to tell me why, but my brother Brian made a similar choice to go into psychiatric nursing (I am not saying that his reasons were the same as mine), and he chose to work at Callan Park.

14

Here is another little niggle. Growing up, we were always told that we had never had any grandparents; they had all died before we were born. It was stated as an unquestionable fact, or rather, an assertion that was not to be questioned. It was easy enough to believe – none of us children ever met a grandparent. When I started on the Modest Quest, my sister began to remember things and she remembered intriguing things. It's amazing what a difference two years in age can make, and perhaps also the fact that she was a girl and I was a boy. She was privy to things that I never knew anything about. Isn't that interesting?

She remembered going on a journey with dad to visit someone when she was about three. (I would have been one year old, and we would have been living at Norm's place.) They went to an institution and visited someone who was old and in a bed. She is not really sure if it was a man or a woman. We have had to struggle with memories; another time she told me that she visited dad's father, and he was in a hospital, and he had no legs. Now I have his death certificate, and it says, as to cause of death (among other things), "peripheral vascular disease, many years". Is that an amazingly understated way of saying, "We had to cut off his legs"?

Was my sister right about how old she was at the time? We discussed this, and this is the only clue. She remembered that on the journey, maybe at a railway station, she needed to go the toilet to do a wee, and she was too young to go into the toilets by herself, so dad had to take her into the men's toilet. So my sister and I had a good laugh about that. We are both parents; we both know that predicament that fathers have, when out alone with a young daughter.

But who was the person my sister visited? Memory only seems to hold impressions; it is not interested in holding a register of incontrovertible facts. From what I know, the best answer is that it was dad's father, and this was the occasion on which she saw an old man who had no legs. In other words, my sister visited her grandfather, who was alive in about 1951. And what do the facts say? Eventually, I tracked the record for his death and bought it, and it was convincingly correct. There is a section on death certificate headed "8. Issue in order of birth, their names and ages", and there was my father: "Sydney J. 42". My father was 42 when his father died, and I was five.

And there was the child I had been searching for for months: "Frances P. 37". Not that the age was accurate. I still had to dig for her date of birth. What it told me was that she was real, and she was alive in 1955. I did find it, Frances's date of birth. It was 9th September 1920. Her mother was admitted to Callan Park on 23 February 1921.

She never came out; she spent the rest of her life in a mental institution.

The other staggering thing came back to me: he was "Married". His wife had gone into an institution in 1920 and he had remained married to her until his death thirty-five years later. And she had been described as "deceased" on numerous marriage certificates in the meantime. This is the rancid smell of sadness and helplessness, laced with anger. I am sure it was, at least in this family's perception, an accepted convention to say that their mother had died, but what a travesty!

I had to wonder, too, what became of this child. That took a while to come to the surface. Looking here and there, I found her marriage, and I found her death. They had three children, but more significantly, I don't know who brought her up.

Frances Phillipa Martin, born 9th September 1920, Arncliffe, died 22 January 2006, Mudgee. Married Leslie John Marks, 1941.

The marriage seemed like an impulsive wartime event. Leslie was a lorry driver, and a Private Buck was one of the witnesses. Frances was not yet twenty-one years old, and her father's consent to the marriage is noted on the marriage certificate. Leslie wasn't much older than Frances; he was twenty-two. Twelve months later, Leslie joined the army. He served out the war in the Malaria Control Unit. I am guessing that the army used him as a lorry driver. Leslie was discharged from the army in early 1946, and he lived until 1976. After that, Frances went to live in Mudgee, a few hours from Sydney, and she lived until 2006, which made her 86, a good long life. It seems like she was in Mudgee because one of her children lived there.

By this time I had discovered another tool, the Australian Cemeteries Index, which, if you are lucky, has photos of headstones that you are looking for. Frances was "a much loved grandmother and great grandmother". Her middle name "Phillipa" was for her own grandmother. It's funny that her first name was Frances, my mother's sister's name. It is as if the two families presage the future. There are several names that crop up in the other sphere a generation or two before a couple encounters one another.

Thomas is a good example. It figures strongly in the Martin family, but it is also the name of my mother's father.

I have enumerated all of my father's siblings. Now I will attempt to do the same for my mother's siblings. And then there are some residual questions.

Chapter 4: My mother's home breaks up

15

I remember asking mum when I was young (maybe ten), about her family and dad's family – how many brothers and sisters did you each have? She said, "There were lots." "How many?" "Oh, maybe ten in both families." "Do you know their names?" "Only some of them." "Why?" "Well, I went to live with Frances when I was about twelve." "Why?" "My parents died."

And that was it. But she did know all of them, and we knew most of them as well. We knew Frances, she was the most familiar sibling, but we also knew Pearl, and Victor, and we had heard of the two boys, Tommy and Jackie. So there were actually six in all, not ten. Which raises the question, why would she say, or think, there were ten?

I think she remembered that that there were "a lot" of brothers and sisters, but that past had been blurred by subsequent events – going to live with Frances at about twelve, and her life in that family then obscuring what had gone before. And I think that there was trauma associated with memories of her early life, so it was an effort to remember exactly who was there; she had to mentally work it out again.

So, in looking for my mother's siblings, I realise I am stepping close to the circumstances of her going to live with Frances. I know that I will need to know something about her two parents in order to find the details about her siblings. There was the complicating issue that most of the children were born after 1914, so I can't simply look up their births in the BDM registry. Marriages should not be so difficult, nor, perhaps, deaths.

Right from the start it was fortunate that I had mum's parents' names, because otherwise, finding Frances would have been tricky. We had always known her as Frances, nothing else, but that was not her name. I don't think that even mum knew her real name, which was "Alice Frances". The registry didn't even state the "Frances" part, it just said "Alice F".

I was fortunate on two counts. First, I had her parents' names and her approximate age, and secondly, I had connected with another family tree, that belonged to a second cousin, twice removed, of my mother's. I am not quick at working out these relationships, but I can plod through slowly and get there.

With that information, I was able to locate Frances's birth in the records, in 1912. She was the first child of the marriage, eleven years older than my mother. A fact of little consequence, you might say. But I was curious about how what I found would relate to mum's memories. We were well-acquainted with the story. Her parents had died when she was twelve, and the family was broken up. Other members of the family took the younger children to live with them.

Frances was married and had a house, so she could manage to take mum. Jackie, the youngest, went to live with Tommy, the second eldest. Mum was lucky; Frances and Norm looked after her well, although they had three young children (all girls) of their own. Mum stayed with them until she got married to dad when she was twenty-three. Tommy was not so lucky; Tommy was harsh, and Jacky got beaten up a lot. He left home in his early teens and found somewhere else to live.

Victor was four years older than mum, so he didn't have to go to another family. Pearl was seven years older than mum, and she was either married or about to be married, so she didn't have to be farmed out either. After finding dates for all mum's siblings' births (or at least, the year in which they were born), I proceeded to find their marriages. I knew the husbands' or wives' names in most cases.

Here is a running account of the siblings' vital details.

Alice Frances (Frances) Archer, born 1912, Marrickville; died 1976, Kingsgrove. Married Norman Leslie Gray at Marrickville, 1934. Three children: Evelyn (1934), Elaine (1937), Noelene (1939).

Thomas (Tommy) James George Archer, born 1914, Marrickville; died (not known). Married Emily Isabelle Lemme at Petersham, 1938. Children: not known.

Florence Pearl (Pearl) Archer, born 1916, Marrickville; died 2003, Toronto, NSW. Married Allen Stanley Brissett at Petersham, 1938. Children: Dorothy, Raymond, Ronald, Valerie. (She divorced Allen later and then married "Zip" Charlton.)

Victor William Archer, born 9 May 1919, Sydney; died 18 August 2015, Bankstown. Married Thelma Ellen May Martin (dad's sister) at Canterbury on 12 July 1941. Children: Joy, Victor, Robert.

Alma Helen (Nell) Archer, born 23 November 1923 at Sydney; alive, November 2016. Married Sydney James Martin (dad) at Campsie, 4 July 1947. Children: Helen (1948), Glenn (1950), Brian (1952).

John (Jackie) Archer, born 22 March 1928, probably also at Marrickville; died 18 July 2009 at Grafton. Married Jean Baker (her surname turned up much later in another family tree), 1959; there were no children.

It is patchy, I know.

16

I want to map mum's remembered experience of what happened when she was growing up against these facts. She remembers Frances's three girls, and that Noelene was still in nappies.

It was 1935 when she was twelve. I had been led to believe that both her parents died when she was twelve, and it was then that the decision was made for her to go and live with Frances. I say "led to believe" because mum has told me this story many times over the years, but when it comes to that critical part, what happened when she was twelve, I don't ever remember her explicitly saying: "both my parents died that year".

I also have to confess that I don't remember what were the actual words she did (or does) use. Memory is a recalcitrant beast. It was just the conclusions I drew from the words she used. She also says that Noelene, Frances and Norm's youngest child, was still in nappies. I do the arithmetic – that makes it 1939 (at the earliest) and mum was sixteen then, not twelve. What is wrong? Which part do I question? That's always the hard part – I know that something doesn't fit, doesn't work, but which part?

Clearly I need to find out the parents' dates of death. And yes, I know from my visit to Woronora Cemetery that the father, Thomas Richard Archer, died on 11 June 1936, and the mother, Margaret Florence Archer, died on 20 March 1941. They did not die at the same time. Mum's father died when she was twelve, that is true, but her mother did not die until five years later. What does that mean? What is the "real" story?

Thomas Archer died of kidney failure and an enlarged prostate. His death certificate notes that mum was twelve. And Margaret Florence Archer died five years later (1941), when mum was seventeen. Mum knows this, or knew it once, because on 20th March 1942, there was an "In memoriam" notice for Margaret Archer in the *Sydney Morning Herald*, submitted by the three girls, Frances, Pearl and Nellie: "In remembrance of our beloved mother, Margaret, who passed away March 20, 1941; also our father, Thomas, who passed away June 11, 1936. Sadly missed."

From the way mum talks about her schooling, and when she had to leave school, I think she went to live with Frances not long after her father's death. Maybe it was Elaine who had just been born, and was in nappies, and Noelene came along later. So maybe it was sometime in 1938. Although, mum is always quite clear about being twelve years of age, or maybe even eleven and a half, which makes it about 1935, and the only child at that stage was Evelyn (who was born in spring, 1934).

What is clear is that there was a family conference, and decisions had to be made. The only reason for this has to be that Margaret, the mother, could not manage the children, and this could even have simply meant she could not manage financially.

Or was it something more, something to do with health? Perhaps she simply could not manage. Day to day, as they say. We forget about people's hearts. Margaret could have loved Thomas and relied upon him. And Thomas, perhaps, was heartbroken because his painting business went bust in the Depression and he could not provide for his family as he wished to (and was expected to do by society).

I notice Thomas's parents' names on the death certificate, James and Alice Archer (and Alice's maiden name is Neil) but that doesn't help at this stage because I know nothing about them. Would knowing something about them help me to understand the heart message about the premature demise of mum's parents? Thomas was 49 when he died, and Margaret was 52.

I started to pay more attention to residential addresses on the certificates. At first this was just too much to take in, but the address can be a luminous clue. In 1936, Thomas Richard Archer died at 14 Gerald Street, Marrickville. This was presumably where the family lived and where most of the children were born.

When she died in 1941, Margaret Florence lived at 9 Henry Street, Leichhardt. The informant on her death certificate was T. Archer, her son, and he lived at 9 Henry Street, Leichhardt. Yes, the mother was living with the son when she died. So this older brother of mum's, who supposedly beat up Jackie on a regular basis, was not only looking after Jackie, he was looking after his mother too.

Tommy got married in 1938. What this means is that he had just got married to Emily, and they lived in a little house (as Google street view reveals), and both Jackie and his mother are assigned to them to take care of. I have no idea what kind of person Tommy was, or his wife, or what their relationship was like. But I can appreciate the enormous strains (both financial and emotional) that may have been imposed on their fledging relationship. At the same time, isn't this what everyone did then – take on the burdens that family might present?

In my ignorance I want to know what precedent there is for this, what kind of family history makes it expected for Tommy and his new wife to pick up the pieces of a recent family tragedy. Yes, big sister Frances was doing her bit too, at a similar stage of life. And yes, there is the social context – what families did for each other in an era when social security was not such a ubiquitous (although rather thin) blanket. And then you feed in personal desires and predilections. Perhaps Tommy had not enjoyed family life while growing up, and had then found a lover to spend his life with, and then the family came clamouring in again.

Did Tommy beat Jackie up? I accept that Jackie had a miserable experience and that he felt the need to run away when he was probably too young to do so. I also know that in those days, authority figures (parents, school teachers) felt obliged to be tough, and to physically discipline those who were in their charge. I accept that it is an appropriate response to run away from this; it is mindless and pointless brutality. But most people are creatures of their context; it is hard to cut away from such beliefs and live in compassion. Most people do what they think they have to do, and what everybody else does.

It made a difference to me to learn that Tommy was also looking after his mother. Before that I was prepared to accept that he was simply resentful of having to look after his little brother, and he was harsh. I don't know what it means, that he was looking after his mother as well, but I have to weigh it up. If he was a real bastard, he would have found a way to slide out of these responsibilities. He had a job, but it was a menial job – he was a tyre fitter at a business underneath one of the railway arches near Central Railway Station, underneath the railway line heading towards the city. You know them? They have been there since before I was born.

Hence, the addresses on death certificates can be quite important, and the stories I have heard from my mother – while I don't doubt their sincerity, I have to question them in the light of what the certificates tell me. Let's say that Tommy is listening here, and I am endeavouring to be fair, while not denying the experience that people have.

In later life, Jackie went to live in Grafton, and that is not so far from Ballina, where my mum lives, and they got back in contact, so I know my mum had affection for Jacky and his life, and she was proud of him. And I remember encountering him at George's funeral (mum's second husband), and recognising him because of the Archer nose.

17

I looked at Google street view to see where the Archer family lived in Marrickville. It is now an industrial area, but there is one house near to number 14 that gives an indication of what the houses were like back in the 1930s. It is a "decent-sized" house, brick, with some ornamental features and two chimneys. I imagine that this is similar to what their house would have been like. It is close to the railway line, and in fact it is closer to Sydenham Station than to Marrickville.

Just down the road, now, is the Gasoline Pony, described in Google street view as "an offbeat spot for craft beers and live music. I have been there to enjoy the craft beer, the live music, and to mill with people for a while. And just across the road, in Gerald Street, one of the industrial buildings sells buttons and is home to an embroidery firm. One of the things mum has told me about her mother is that she did beautiful crochet, and my mother is a dressmaker, so there are nice resonances there about how life has moved on.

Thomas Richard Archer died of kidney disease. He was a smoker. I know this, not from anything mum said, but from the fact that mum has a single photograph of him and in it he is holding a cigarette. It is not a formal shot taken in a studio. He is outside, sitting on a box, dressed in white overalls and with other men standing behind him in white overalls. Mum said that this was when he owned a painting business, and these men were his workers.

Margaret Florence Archer died of carcinoma of the stomach. I wonder if she smoked too. I am learning a little about medical facts, and it seems that stomach cancer is much more common in men than women, but also, that smoking is a factor. I also think that in the 1930s, stomach cancer took a rapid trajectory, so I suspect that she did not have it in 1936, when her husband died. But perhaps she had other medical problems, and this led to the split-up of the children.

I am trying to pin a date on when mum went to live with Frances. She was twelve when Thomas Archer died, but it was twelve months later that Elaine was born, and Noelene wasn't born until two years after that. The scenario that makes best sense to me is that mum went to live with Frances just after Elaine was born. Elaine was the one in nappies. Noelene was born when mum was already living there.

Why has this become tangled in mum's mind (because I think that is what has happened)? I think it is partly because of trauma. My dad died when I was sixteen, and I think I was part numb for about two years, so there would have been lots of things that happened during that time that I missed or misread. Mum tells me now that she loved her father; he was a lovely, gentle man. Mum's dad died when she was twelve, and she had to move house soon after because her mother was unable to look after the family and the household. She would have been experiencing great uncertainty as well as sorrow, and perhaps felt that she was a burden to her big sister.

And also, I have noticed over a period of many years, that as mum has got older, some of the facts in the stories get compressed. I mean, she might have told me two different stories twenty years ago, and now they have been compressed into one set of facts, combining people or skipping twenty years.

Mum left school before she completed her Intermediate Certificate, which you generally completed when you were fifteen in those days. She worked for a while at the mill where many of the Archers worked. But before too long she got the opportunity to learn dressmaking, and that got her out of the factory. She also took up her Intermediate again at night school.

18

I am thinking again of the story that people in our family die before they are fifty. Looking at all her siblings, and how long they lived, the evidence is seriously lacking. Again, I do the arithmetic – how long did they each live for? Frances, 64; Tommy – having searched the records and not found him, I believe he was still alive in 1984, so he lived to be at least 70; Pearl, 87; Victor, 96; Jackie, 81; and mum is still alive at 93.

The question is: how many events does it take to make a myth? I think the answer is: just your own two parents, more or less. Realising this really brought it home to me what a powerful effect family events can have on young children, for a lifetime. And doing the work on uncovering the correct information about all these people has had a powerful effect too, on me. The ideas that take hold of us when we don't know about something can grow very large and intransigent.

This is true of general social beliefs as well, such as "people had large families then", meaning every period of time before about 1950. Or, "men went to work and women stayed at home and were housewives". Even if the assertions are true generally, they may not necessarily be true of your family. Yes, both mum and dad came from large families – six children in each family. But was this true of all generations going back? And I note that my mum always worked. She did dressmaking. You could argue, I suppose, that she was a housewife too, because she worked from home, but what about her female predecessors? Were they all "housewives" or did they have occupations?

I am afraid that my questions are already over-reaching. They are the kind of questions that would not be addressed in a modest quest to name your parents' siblings. I still had the urge to find out more, because even at this generational level, there were myths from mum that I had not been able to test. For example, she said, many of the Archers were nurses or teachers, so it would make sense if that's what we turned to be.

We did in fact, in our generation, turn out to be nurses and teachers. My explanation is that mum's myth was the best vocational guidance we got. I went to a vocational guidance centre when I was in high school, and they tested me for a day, and at the end of it they said, "You can do anything you want. You have the intelligence." Well, that was no advice at all, was it? I had no idea about any occupations apart from my parents and school. But how many of mum's relatives were nurses or school teachers?

I don't know what trade or occupation Tommy had (well, now I do; he was a tyre fitter). Mum's sisters were indeed housewives; they all had three or four children and a husband who had a job. Victor and Jackie had their own stories, but neither were teachers. Victor was clever; he was an accountant. When young, he worked in the office at a manufacturing firm but he was interested in the manufacturing process too, and he invented something. He left and set up his own manufacturing business making taps for beer and for petrol bowsers, and that business served him for a lifetime. He passed it onto his son.

After his bad early start in life, Jackie got himself a job with the Sydney City Council, and learned how to be a gardener. However, after a few years of that, he and his wife left and went north, all the way to the top end of Queensland. They lived on beaches for several years, but they were not idle. They began to collect shells. Gradually they put together a massive collection of shells and sea creatures. They came back to Sydney and acquired the use of an old ambulance station near Sutherland and housed the collection there.

Jackie's shell collection attracted busloads of people, both adults and school-children, to look at the wonders he had gathered up north, and this business kept him going for many years. The collection consisted of more than 3,000 shells as well as a crocodile skin, a giant clam that was nearly a metre across, and a deadly stonefish. There were also native artefacts from Queensland and New Guinea – throwing spears, axes, grass skirts and wood carvings.

Mum had a newspaper clipping from the local paper (Sutherland) in June 1964 that was an article about Jackie and his collection. It was headed "Beauty and death lay side by side", referring to the juxtaposition of the exquisite shells and the stonefish. She gave the article to me, which was a nice acknowledgment of my project, because I was always a bit wary talking about the project with mum. She had these mythologies that were fixed truths for her, and I wasn't sure what some of them were based on, and I was discovering that some of them were based on flimsy or very little evidence. Were my family history investigations a threat, that I was testing the truth of these myths?

There were also subjects that she was clearly unwilling to talk about, subjects that were uncomfortable for her, and even taboo to bring up. I had learned that when quite young, and it hasn't changed much now. Dad's mother was the principal subject of taboo. As soon as I got close to that I could see her stiffen up. It had something to do with the last baby, Francie.

There were also assertions (myths) that were repeated regularly, and in some cases, in word-for-word fashion. For example, she often said, and adamantly, that "All the Archers came to Australia as free settlers. None of them were convicts." When I was growing up, that distinction between convicts and free settlers still persisted, softened with the passage of generations but still indicating that there had been a strong and vociferous social divide amongst Australia's citizens, based on how your ancestors got here in the first place.

But for now, I am dealing with one thing at a time, and I will get to the next thing in good time.

Eventually Jackie sold the whole shell collection and went up to Grafton, with his wife, to live out his days. Mum says that he starting keeping rare birds, parrots and the like, and did some trade in them.

Where are the school teachers and nurses?

19

There is indeed a nurse, just one, as far as I know (apart from my sister), but she is of considerable stature. There were just three newspaper articles that mum kept. The first was about her younger brother Jackie, and the other two were about the Matron of Darwin Hospital, Matron Brennan, dated March and May, 1978. Matron Brennan was Miss Lorraine Brennan. She was the daughter of Aunty Dolly, meaning, in this instance, that Aunty Dolly was my mum's aunt, being her father's youngest sister. So Lorraine was my mother's cousin.

On another occasion, mum told me that Aunty Dolly had been a twin, but her twin sister had died at birth. This is relevant because I have twin sons. When they were born, the first thing family members do is go on the hunt for other twins in the family, so they can tell you on whose side the other twins were, and how many generations they go back. As it turns out, and, I think, unsurprisingly, there were twins on my wife's side too, as it has been reported to me. There were also twins on my father's side, not just my mother's.

There was more to it as well. Aunty Dolly and her twin sister were not the only set of twins in her family. Aunty Dolly was the last child in the family, born in 1899; her mother was 37 then. But altogether there were twelve children born to James and Alice Archer, and the third and fourth were twins, born in 1885. They both died the same year; perhaps they both died at birth. Which is to say, there were two sets of twins born to the same parents.

In telling you this, I might as well confess that there are now over 3,000 people in the family tree, far more than the dozen or so people I was initially committed to finding. One thing leads to another. In order to understand my parents' siblings, I had to find out about their parents, and in any case the parents were not far away. I had names and some details, I just had to find out the rest. And in some cases there were questions beckoning anyway, like the question about dad's mum.

Oh well, "In for a penny, in for a pound".

After I was talking to mum one Sunday night about (carefully selected parts of) the family history, she wrote me a letter with more details that she remembered. Lorraine Brennan was "Laurie" Brennan, and Mum said she was "2 or 3 years older" than her. There is endless amusement in the niceties of memory and our remembered impressions. I do have the birth details for Laurie. She was born on 23

February 1923, while my mum was born in November of the same year. They were less than twelve months apart. But Laurie must have seemed older to mum for some reason.

Anyway, Laurie became a nurse and she went up to Darwin, eventually becoming the Matron of the hospital. She was devoted to her work and she was well-respected. She was the Matron there in 1974, the year that Darwin was almost completely destroyed by a cyclone. Most Australians who are old enough know about Cyclone Tracy. It happened on Christmas Eve, 1974 during the tumultuous and exciting years of the Whitlam Government. Darwin was a small city a long way away from all other major cities in Australia, a city of about 50,000 people on Australia's northern coast, with thousands of kilometres of desert stretching around it to the south.

Matron Brennan was not the only family member who lived there. A cousin, Aunty Pearl's daughter Valerie, had gone there to live with her husband, and they had three small children, one of them a baby of about six months of age. I think her husband worked for the government. I'm not positive about the details of all this, but the gist of it is true. About the following story, I have two sources. The first is mum – she is in the story as a witness, and the other source is a website on Cyclone Tracy.

It was Christmas Eve, and people were getting ready for Christmas – presents, trees, decorations, food and beer. But there was also a cyclone looming up in the north. People were a little wary. Darwin had had damaging cyclones before, but at the same time, it meant that people had experience; a cyclone was not unprecedented. People did make preparations for the cyclone, and the hospital made preparations too, stocking up on extra supplies, including blood for transfusions.

By late afternoon, the city was covered with heavy, low cloud and there were patches of rain and gusts of wind. But it was around 10 pm that the wind got stronger, enough to start causing damage to houses. The cyclone had hit, and it continued for over six hours, tearing the roofs off houses and ripping down their walls, battering them to the ground and hauling their debris up into the air. In many areas of the city, every building was smashed, and overall, more than 90 percent of the city was destroyed in that one night. The houses were not built for this kind of ferocity.

In their house, Valerie, her husband John and their two young children took refuge, firstly under a table, but the wind blew the glass out of all the windows of the house, and then the house started to break up. It was a high-block, fibro house with space underneath, designed to keep the house cooler in summer, and it was no match for this savage wind. Downstairs there was a laundry built against a brick wall, and they thought they would be safest near to that wall, if John parked their utility right up against the wall and they stayed inside that.

When they went out to descend, most of the stairs had disappeared already and they had to jump. Valerie was wounded by flying debris, but they made it into the back of the utility and they lay there in the dark in terror the whole night, doing what parents do, sheltering their children, in the midst of the deafening roar of the wind, the sound of houses smashing around them, and flying debris crashing into things. Valerie said that the noise never let up the entire time, except for the brief, dreaded time when you enter the eye of the storm, and then it comes back the other way with vengeance. (Mum was quite clear about this whole story.)

The city's electricity and communications failed during the night, and it took a series of improvisations to get news of the disaster to the outside world the next morning, Christmas Day. Officials in Canberra learned of the disaster during the morning but it was lunch time before the extent of the situation was clear, and it was the afternoon before news reached the Australian public, saying that "the city's plight was grave".

People who had cars started leaving town on the road south, heading for towns along the highway, or heading for Adelaide. The airport was still operational, as was the hospital. From early morning, patients began arriving at the hospital, suffering lacerations from flying glass, broken bones and bruises. Over sixty people had died during the cyclone. During the day, more than 500 patients were treated. The hospital's two operating theatres worked non-stop all day on Christmas Day, and halfway into the night. Two teams of doctors arrived from Canberra on Boxing Day to relieve the Darwin doctors.

There were about 30,000 people crammed into emergency centres and makeshift housing, without water, electricity or sanitation. Major-General Stretton, head of a recently established National Disasters organisation, flew into Darwin and began to coordinate relief efforts, including the mass evacuation of people who were wounded.

Valerie and her children were part of the evacuations by plane, but it was three days before they could get out, and during that whole time, Valerie's mother Pearl did not know if they were dead or alive. Communications were not what they are today. Husband John stayed in Darwin to help with the rescue and recovery operations. When mum found out about the disaster in Darwin, she got on the bus and went straight over to Pearl's house and together they waited.

She said it was late afternoon on the third day, about four o'clock, when there was a knock on the door and a policeman was there. He had brought Valerie and the two children from the airport. The plane had flown from Darwin to Sydney with a full load of refugees. Valerie and the kids were wearing big identification tags, Valerie was bandaged up from her wounds, and they were all still wearing the clothes they had been wearing on the night of the cyclone. Mum said they all just burst into tears and fell into each others' arms.

There was lots of family sympathy for Valerie. She was one of those robust, cheerful people – she always had been so as a child. And she married her love when she was young, maybe nineteen. I remember the wedding. She was close to my sister's age, a little bit older than me. But it was the time of the Vietnam War, that is, Australia's military involvement in Vietnam, and soon after their marriage her husband, Peter, was conscripted. Thence followed a quick stint at Puckapunyal army training base in Victoria and in no time at all he was shipped off to Vietnam. He was part of an engineering corps. But he had been in Vietnam no more than six weeks when he was killed, blown up when a mine hit the truck he was travelling in.

So, at about age twenty, Valerie had been married and then had suddenly become a widow. It was shocking, it was dreadful, and it was extraordinarily sad. I had not experienced much death around me when I was growing up, with the notable exception of my father when I was sixteen. Valerie's husband's death sent shudders through me. It was close, it was part of known family. And in addition, it was different from dad's death – he had died of natural causes, while this was a violent death, in war. We had been swept up into world events over which we had no control.

In the light of this history, everyone was pleased when she met this fellow John a couple of years later and they got married. There was also a point of resonance about the fact that they went to live in Darwin where another known relative was living, Matron Brennan. Valerie and her husband were committed to living in Darwin. When the city was rebuilt, they went back there to live, and Valerie lived there until she died about thirty years later.

Matron Brennan must have worked as hard as those doctors in the operating theatre on Christmas Day, all day and into the night. There was so much to think about, and manage. She was looking after the hospital itself, but also about twenty temporary medical centres that had been set up around the destroyed city. She had to make sure that patients could flow through to somewhere else safe after they had been treated. She had to organise the additional doctors and nurses who were coming in on planes from the south to help. She had to coordinate with the authorities who were worried about the risk of disease breaking out, especially in the hot and humid conditions.

The website on Cyclone Tracy says that "by 27 December it was judged that the immediate health emergency was under control", despite the fact that the interim coordinating committee agreed that "Darwin had, for the time being, ceased to exist as a city".

My mother told me that Laurie Brennan was awarded the MBE (Member of the British Empire) for her efforts during the cyclone crisis. The two newspaper articles, the first from March 1978, report that she was named as Woman of the Year by the Quota Club of Darwin, "in recognition of many services in excess of her daily duties". No mention is made of Cyclone Tracy. But there had to be a list online of MBE recipients, so I searched for that, and indeed there was. But here is the surprise: Matron Brennan was awarded the MBE in 1971, three years before the cyclone.

Laurie Brennan became the matron of Darwin Hospital in 1965, so she had obviously served the hospital, and the city, effectively and devotedly, in the years to 1971. Once again I am fascinated about how events become compressed and "simplified", if you like, over time. And in this case, it seems perfectly appropriate.

There was another story about Laurie Brennan. In browsing other family trees I found mention of a man in relation to Laurie Brennan. I say I "found mention" because it didn't seem to be saying she was married to this man, who is identified only by a surname, "Miller". But did she retire and then marry a man in later life? She came back to Sydney and she died at Eastwood when she was sixty-nine. I asked mum, and she did know the answer to this question.

There had been a man when she was young, and mum thought they had been engaged to be married. But then the war (the Second World War) happened; it was 1939 and he must have joined the army, or he was already in the army. In any case, he went off to war and he was killed, and after that, Laurie never married. She devoted herself to nursing. I have come across one other instance of this in the family quest, a young woman who loves a man who goes off to war and gets killed, and the woman never marries.

So strange, sad and unsettling. Does this happen today? Do people (women or men) still do this? It makes me think of a song that Missy Higgins wrote, that has the line: "our hearts are fierce". I think there must be a fierceness to a heart that decides to continue to love another who is gone forever.

I started to wonder where I was at the time of Cyclone Tracy. It's not hard to figure it out. I had got married during 1974, and our first child, Elvina, was born in November. She was six weeks premature, so we were engrossed by the carefulness required with a very small baby, beyond the wonder and new responsibilities of parenthood. On top of that, I was working as a psychiatric nurse at Parramatta Psychiatric Centre, having left teaching. However, I had applied for a job as a teacher in Queensland, and at Christmas time I was waiting to hear whether I had been appointed to a position, and where we would be going. I found out in the third week of January that I had been appointed to Mackay North High School, another city prone to cyclones. I had one week to organise to move myself and our little family 1,800 kilometres.

20

I can remember some of the stories mum has told me about her early adulthood. Although she lived in inner city suburbs, she and friends did venture outside of Sydney into the country. One haunt was the Burragorang Valley, before Warragamba Dam was built and it became part of the catchment area, permanently flooded. They used to go there bushwalking and horse-riding. She told me this story.

They went out horse-riding in a group of about twelve, with the man who looked after the horses. It all went fine with mum until they had to ford a stream, and her horse baulked. It stepped into the shallow water and simply stopped. Nothing mum said or did would make it move. The instructor said, "That's it. You'll never get that horse to do anything now." He got mum to dismount and they swapped horses. Things went fine after that.

There's a lesson there about horses and how to work with them.

Mum also told me that she went out with a man who owned a motor bike. She knew that Frances's husband, Norm, would disapprove of that, so when the man brought her home on the motor bike, late one night, they played it safe and he let her off about a block from home. The next morning Norm said to mum, sternly, "You've been out with that fellow with the motor bike again." It was an English Triumph with a big thumping engine. Sound carried a long way in those days late on silent suburban nights.

Norm used to play piano and during the war he played at a lot of night-time events, events to keep up the spirits of the civilian populace, and events to entertain US soldiers spending time (and money) in Sydney. Apart from that he sold rope for a living.

Mum had volunteer jobs during the war, as well as knitting to send care packages to soldiers overseas. Some nights she worked in a canteen. Canteens were social venues for soldiers and girls happy to meet them and have a laugh. She also served at a smart restaurant, Cahill's. "Cahill's", she told me, "not Coles". There were lots of occasions where young people went out as a group, whether it was a dance or a bushwalk or some other entertainment. In the midst of the fear and uncertainty of war, it seems that they had their ways of staying sane.

21

I am not sure if I have satisfactorily resolved the question of what happened following my mother's father death in 1936. I ended up doing a head count of the relevant people from around that time. I started with this question: where were all the members of the Archer family when Thomas Richard died in June 1936?

Wife Margaret Florence is alive and present. Here is my account of all the children:

- Frances (24): has left home, having married Norm Gray in 1934; they have one child, Evelyn; Elaine will be born next year, then Noelene the following year;

- Tommy (22): he may have left home; he marries Emily Lemme in 1938, and both Jackie and mother Margaret end up living with him;
- Pearl (20): she may have left home; she marries Allen Brissett in 1937;
- Victor (16): he is probably still at home (he gets married to Thelma Martin three months after his mother dies in 1941);
- Helen A. (mum)(12): at home;
- John D. (Jackie)(7): at home.

Having done this, I still think that mum and Jackie stayed with their mother for a while after their father's death. I am not sure who else was at home, except that I am certain that Victor was. Mum talks about things that she and Jackie did with Victor as kids, playing and adventures, and Victor was a pragmatic person who would have ensured his own stability while he finished his education. Victor was the one who eventually started his own business. And if Victor had gone to another family member to live, mum would have remembered this vividly. Victor was also the one who married Thelma Martin, when he was twenty-two, and Thelma had a brother called Sid, my father.

I don't pursue this enquiry any further, because I think I have fathomed what I can about the situation. What this picture tells me is that, as a younger sibling, mum experienced the continual loss of bigger brothers and sisters, as they left home and went out into the world. She was losing the family that had always been around her as a child. And then her father died as well. I can see that this would shake her up and disturb her.

As children, we are not so robust. Our experiential world is small, and everything that happens in it is correspondingly big. Adults have more experiences, so we have many more reference points that enable us to put things into context and make sense of what is happening at the moment. It's as if we have a bigger footprint so we are more solid on the ground. So then I wonder about my father's childhood.

Chapter 5: My father's home breaks up

22

Mum said to me, in another conversation about family history, "Your father was brought up by his Aunty Maud". And I thought, "Who? Why?" But then I realised that this was connected with the story about dad's mother. I had found dad's younger sister, Frances, the one that was born in September 1920, followed by the mother's admission to Callan Park Mental Hospital in February 1921. But I hadn't got to following through on the consequences of this for my father.

I do the arithmetic: he was just six. How serious was this admission to Callan Park? Did his mother come back home? If not, something had to have happened about caring for dad.

Just as I did above for my mother at the time of her father's death, now I attempt a head count of all the relevant people in February 1920. Elizabeth Hannah Martin was 38 years old when she was admitted to Callan Park. Her husband William Thomas was 37. They had six children (Albert had died as a baby):

- Norman William was eleven;
- William Thomas was nine;
- Sydney James (dad) was six;
- George Edwin was five;
- Thelma Ellen was two (one month short of her third birthday);
- Frances, the baby, was five months old.

In other words, all of the children were young enough to be dependent, not even old enough to get a job, even in those days when children might leave school at thirteen and get a job. There were no older children, as in mum's family, who could take on the care of a younger sibling. What happened to the household, and if it was broken up, where did the children go?

Mum had given me part of the answer – at least dad left the household, and he was cared for by an older relative, so the mother's admission into the mental hospital must have been serious, that is, of considerable duration. I didn't know who Aunty Maud was yet. I had tracked a lot of dad's father's siblings, and had some births, dates and places. I had the feeling that I would have to find out a lot more before I could tell a coherent life story of my parents. And the great bogey of family history investigations was staring at me too, saying, "You don't really have the full story of a person until you know who their parents were", and of course, this story never ends, because everyone has two parents, who are necessary if you are to understand the person, and each of them has two parents too.

I could ignore it if I thought that the next generation would be the same. If I could say, my father was a painter and he was born in an inner suburb of Sydney, and he had several brothers and sisters, that would be fine. That would be a satisfactory end to it, especially if I thought that all the previous generations were similar – all born in the same locality, and if the men weren't all painters, at least they were all trades people.

Alternatively, the trail would go back a couple of generations and then fade into obscurity for lack of records. That would be an end that I could accept as well. But now I have a pile of unexplained facts, and every new piece of information raises new questions. I have a mental health crisis of some kind, with dad's mum, that I have no explanation for, and it looks as if it is serious enough to have led to the splitting up of the family. I can't drop this with the excuse that the answers are impossible to find, that there are no records, because I know that if dad's mum was in a mental institution, there are records. They would still exist, they would be in a box somewhere, and with enough effort, I could get my hands on those records. So this was like seeing myself at the bottom of a hill, and the hill looked very steep. But the hill was there; it would not go away.

I could explain, well enough, I think, why I grew up thinking that both my mother's parents died at the same time, but I always thought that both dad's parents had died well before I was born, and that has turned out to be not true. At school, if the subject came up, I would say we had no grandparents, that we had never had any grandparents. They had all died before I was born. Occasionally someone would say, "What, all of them?" and I would say, "Yes, all of them", because that was an unquestionable fact.

It took me months to find dad's father's date of death (which had occurred when I was five) and obtain his death certificate. For dad's mum, I simply never found her until after I learned that she was admitted to Callan Park.

There is a practical reason why "you don't really have the full story of a person until you know who their parents were". When you look up deaths in the BDM registry, the clues you have are the date of death, the name of the person, and the first names of the person's parents. The name "William Thomas Martin" is very common. During the period that "my" William Thomas Martin was alive, there were sixteen others in New South Wales. At least I was reasonably certain that we were only dealing with New South Wales. Having the first names of the parents would be helpful in narrowing the field.

When I added the assumption that he was still alive in 1947, according to my parents' marriage certificate, but that he died before I was born in 1950, that left two or three possibilities. I needed parents' first names. But I also had doubts now about the assumptions I was making. If he didn't die before 1950, he could have lived for many more years. And there is always the issue of whether the names on the registry index are correct. These records have been transcribed from hand-written records in many cases, and sometimes the transcription is in error. For example, I had the name "Deleuil" (which it will take me a while to get to) and it was written in the registry record as "Delenil".

I looked at records of death for William Thomas Martin up to the 1970s, and that yielded a few further possibilities. But I needed to do more than take random stabs at names. I should note that I have a considerable folder now of "Wrong persons". Each one cost me $20 or $30, and at first I would be cranky about the "waste of money". Then I would remember Aunty Dolly and the tens of thousands of dollars she probably spent on her expedition to the mother country to search out records. I had to be prepared to make mistakes. Sometimes those mistakes were essential in getting to the real story.

One benefit of doing this wide search and coming up with numerous possibilities, some before and some after 1950, was that I got accustomed to the idea that I may have had a grandparent I didn't know about when I was a young child. I wondered about the reasons for our not knowing. Was there something shameful about him? Was there simply a general curtain across the realm of the ancestors, because my parents didn't know much about them, or hadn't had much to do with them beyond their early childhood?

My mum wrote me a letter after one of our discussions, correcting a mistake she had made while talking to me on the phone. She said Sid's parents were William Thomas Martin and Elizabeth Eggleston; she copied these names off her marriage certificate for me. I think she had to look at the certificate to be sure. So I think it is quite true that dad's parents were not part of her and dad's lives. Not knowing anything about the mother yet, except that there had been an episode involving her admission to Callan Park in 1920, I am thinking mainly about the father.

I look again at mum's marriage certificate. I am interested in the witnesses now. My understanding is that it is traditional for there to be one witness from each family – the bride's father and the groom's mother, or some such combination. On mum and dad's certificate, the two witnesses are Jean Gray and V. W. Archer. Jean Gray was Frances's husband's sister, and the second witness was mum's older brother, Victor. Given that both of mum's parents were indeed dead in 1947, having her older brother as witness seems appropriate. Yet the second witness is no one from dad's side of the family – not the father, whom we guess is still alive, not his older brother, Norm, or either of his other two brothers, or an uncle, an aunt (Aunty Maud?) or a friend. What am I to make of this?

This is dad's second marriage, so maybe that makes it different from a first marriage. I go back to his first marriage, when he married Olive Coates at age twenty-one. In this case, both the witnesses are from Olive's family. I think, was my father that alone? The two witnesses are Olive's brother-in-law, Wally Becker, and Olive's mother. I notice that this marriage is in a Catholic church, St Fiacre's at Leichhardt. Am I looking at estrangement here? Did dad's family disapprove of him marrying a Roman Catholic? Did this disapproval continue when he married mum, ten years later?

The question of when dad's father died had to sit and wait until I had filled in enough other parts of the picture. Eventually I found both of William Thomas's parents, who came along with a swag of new questions. William Thomas's father was Thomas, and his mother was Phillipa. Knowing this made it easy to pick out the right death record from the possibilities I had, and I bought the certificate. When the certificate arrived, I read it through carefully. He died on 16th December 1955. It was confirmation that I had had a living grandparent. This radically changed the way I looked at my past.

At the time of his death, William Thomas Martin was in Lidcombe State Hospital, just a few miles away from us at Greenacre; he was seventy-two. I remembered that Lidcombe was also the place where dad's two children from his first marriage went to live after Olive died. They were living with Olive's sister, Aunty Dorrie. This connected back to the story my sister had told me – that she had gone with dad and they had visited a man in a big institutional building, and the man was old and he had no legs. Looking at a map of this part of Sydney, you see that it is only five train stations from Wiley Park, where we were living prior to 1954, to Lidcombe, so dad could have taken Helen along with him one day on a trip to visit both his father and his two children.

The informant for William Thomas Martin's death was dad's older brother Norm (N. Martin), 96 Renown Avenue, Punchbowl (which is next to Wiley Park), and this was the place where we had lived until I was four.

23

I am still trying to answer the question, what happened to the Martin household after 1920, and who brought up dad? I know where the father ended up, but what happened before that? And how did he end up there at the hospital?

Months went by, and I focused on finding more relatives in dad's family: if you can't identify a particular thing, surround it until the thing almost has to pop out.

I managed to identify all of dad's fathers' siblings. It wasn't easy, because at some point I crossed the border into Victoria. Dad's father (William Thomas) was not born in New South Wales, he was born in Victoria, in 1883. At some point the family had come to Sydney, because the young man William Thomas was married at St Peters in 1908, and his bride, Elizabeth Hannah Eaglestone, had been born in Balmain. She was a Sydney girl, and he was a Sydney fellow now.

The place in Victoria was also a mystery: Bethanga. I had never heard of it. Consulting Wikipedia, I learned that Bethanga is a mining town in north-eastern Victoria, not far from Albury, on the border with New South Wales. It was a gold-mining town. Gold had been first discovered around 1852, but the main period of gold mining was from 1876, when a gold-bearing reef of quartz was discovered.

Thus I learn that William Thomas Martin was born in a gold-mining town, and he had left there soon after 1900, as a seventeen-year-old. Wikipedia says that the gold began to peter out in the early 1900s. There were quite a few children, girls and boys, and all of them were born in Bethanga. William Thomas Martin's father was Thomas Martin, married to Phillipa. They had many children, and I found details of all of them: Mary Ann

(1879), Frances Matilda (1881), then our William Thomas (1883), then Martha (1885), Thomas (1887), Elizabeth (1889), Stella May (1893), Norman (1895), Paul (1896), Olive (1899) and Egbert Albert (1900).

Thomas and Phillipa Martin didn't bring all of their children with them to Sydney. The younger ones came (like William Thomas), but the older ones stayed behind and some of them got married there. I think there are still Martin families in and around Bethanga, and Martin genes in quite a few other families.

One of the children who came to Sydney was Paul. Where was he in 1920? I found out. He had just got married, to Maud Eustace, who, curiously, was born in Chiltern, another small gold-mining town in Victoria, just down the road from Bethanga (seventy kilometres). Her parents were both born in Chiltern, and they both died in Victoria, so how did Paul and Maud meet, and how did Maud get to Sydney? I don't know the answer to those questions. I suspect that after Thomas and Phillipa Martin came to city, there were family visits back to the old town.

This is what I learned: Paul and Maud got married in 1919, and they had two children, Paul (1921) and Lola (1923). And sometime after February 1920, my father came to live with them, Uncle Paul and Aunty Maud. Was my father welcome, or was he just a duty and a burden? He was a six-year-old boy in distress who had probably just been separated from his older brothers and his younger sisters, as well as not knowing what had happened to his mother. He may have been withdrawn or he may have been acting out in anger.

I try to visualise the context again. Here is William Thomas Martin, in his late thirties, father of six children, aged from eleven down to new-born, after his wife has gone into a mental institution. He is a blacksmith. I am not quite sure what this means in inner Sydney in 1920, but later I read the probate for his will, and it is clear that he worked for an engineering or manufacturing firm, and today he would probably be called a metal worker or a mechanical engineer. At his death, among his estate were ten shares in an engineering firm, worth twenty pounds – no fortune, but an indication that he had an interest in the firm rather than merely being an employee.

The family lived in their own house, a small house for that many children, and William Thomas has to work five or six days a week to keep things going financially. How does a man in a situation like this, at this period of history, survive and provide and care for young children? There had to have been a family conference to discuss options, and who could assist. We can imagine that young Paul and his new wife were not the only people to be called upon. Who else was around?

William Thomas had older sisters, but they were in Victoria. But younger sister Stella May was in Sydney (she was 27; she got married to John Sanderson in 1921). I thought Norman, another sibling, who was a year older than Paul, would have been in Sydney too, but he was not; he was back in Victoria, and would soon get married to a girl who was born at Chiltern. (Had they known each other as young children?) There was Olive Myrtle (21), who also got married around this time. She married Albert Fuller in Newtown in 1921. And there was Egbert, who was just twenty in 1920; he got married to Ellen Chappelow in 1923.

Thinking of who might be a likely carer and doing a tally, we have just two younger sisters of William Thomas (Stella and Olive), but neither of them is yet married in 1920 and they may have been still living with their parents. I wanted to look at the parents too – were they a possibility as carers for one or more of their grandchildren? I also needed to think about Elizabeth Martin's relatives, the Eaglestones.

24

Elizabeth Martin was born Elizabeth Hannah Eaglestone in 1882 in Balmain. Did she have siblings who might have looked after dad's two younger sisters, Thelma and Frances? The Eaglestones are a huge subject in themselves. I have introduced them already – the graves of Edwin and Ellen Eaglestone, carved in sandstone, are at Woronora Cemetery. They remind me of a sunny day of exploration and discovery in the company of my youngest son.

For our current purposes, in 1920 Elizabeth had one sister living: Blanche. Her other sister, Sarah Ellen, had married Herbert Lappan in 1902, had four children in the space of a few years, then died suddenly in 1910, aged twenty-five. Blanche had married another Herbert, Herbert Augustus Royall, in 1904, had nine children, and in 1920 she had walked out of the home. Her husband had initiated divorce proceedings. She is not a likely candidate as a carer for the two young children of William Thomas Martin.

Nevertheless, there was Ellen, Elizabeth's mother. What about her, although she was sixty-three and her husband had died in 1916? I suspect that she was not in the best of health, but that is part of the Eaglestone story. And there were William Thomas's parents too, Thomas and Phillipa. They were both in their early sixties too, although they may have still had four or even five children at home, aged from twenty to twenty-seven, the ones who were not married yet.

I think that Thomas and Phillipa are serious possibilities as the carers of Thelma and Frances. They lived at 29 Station Street Arncliffe, which is a large, solid brick home not far from the station. I am getting the sense that they had status in Bethanga before they migrated to Sydney, and a record of service in the community. But I have nothing further to go on, unless mum can tell me something.

There is also an aunty and two cousins of Elizabeth, who appear when I start exploring the hospital records. But Aunty Sarah (Lappan) is sixty-six and her husband has died too. I feel like I am going around trying to find someone to look after the girls. The two cousins are both daughters of Sarah. They are about the same age as Elizabeth. They are both married. Nellie has one child, a daughter born in 1912; Maggie has three children, aged from thirteen to eight (in 1920).

All of these people lived in the vicinity, within a few kilometres. Would a family ask a cousin to take in, to take on, two very young children? I don't know. But someone looked after them, because both of them grew up, got married and had children, and lived long lives. Thelma lived to ninety-one, and Frances was eighty-six.

Postscript: I spoke to mum. I wished her a happy birthday: ninety-two. I talked about Victor, her brother, so it led to talking about who brought up Thelma, his wife. Her answer was, "her aunty". Should I take this literally? Everyone used to be aunty; they just had to be female and older than you. I asked her if it was the same aunty that brought up dad. No, it wasn't. So, who have we got? It suddenly looks like it could be Sarah, Sarah Philipson. Another confession: I have done a lot of homework, and Sarah Philipson has loomed as a very important person, a pivotal person, in my mind, in the larger tapestry of "the family".

It seems unlikely; she is sixty-six, too old to be taking on the care of young children. But I have a flash of her at age eleven, showing up at the Births, Deaths and Marriages Registry in Sydney, twice: first, to report the birth of her little brother, John Sydney. And she has to turn up a second time, ten days later, to report his death. This is adult business, not an eleven-year-old's. I understand that her mother is indisposed, and she is also illiterate, and intimidated by such things, for that reason alone, apart from the hugeness of what she is dealing with, but where is the father, Edward? Why is he not the one reporting the events?

So it is still an open possibility to me, until I find out more or until I find out otherwise, that Sarah took on the girls, at age sixty-six. I have huge respect for her already, so it within the bounds of possibility.

That's all I can offer to date on the subject of mum and dad's siblings. I have determined who they all are, their dates of birth, marriage and death, and something about the shape of their lives. There is more to be said about William Thomas and Elizabeth Martin, but that belongs in their own story.

One more note on mum's brother, Victor. He died on 18th August 2015. This is how my information came about. Mum told me that Victor always sent her a card at Christmas time, but he hadn't done so for the last two years, so she thought he must have died. She had said this to me a few times over the last two years, and I had the thought more than once that I should be able to find out, with my internet skills! Recently, after one of these conversations, I finally did a search.

Victor had died just one week before. It showed up in a posting on a funerals website. He was ninety-five. Like mum, he was a great grandparent, and like mum, he was the parent of three children. I got a screenshot of the notice, printed it out and posted it to mum, which she appreciated. When I spoke to her next, she said, "Well, I am the last one of my generation alive now. Who would have thought that I would live this long?"

Mmm. We don't know, do we? We wake up in the morning and we are alive. The trick seems to be, to keep on waking up.

25

After my parents' generation (Generation One) there is more, and it is breaking open. It swarms in, disorderly, like clouds, or children in a schoolyard. It is made up of questions, where the answers come attached to more questions. I have to continue, but I do so in wonder. All this I did not know.

I would like to be orderly about this, but it is not going to be like that. I will have to take what comes as it comes, and hope to be able to accommodate it. I wonder how much my head can hold, and whether it will all end up being just a pile of fragments, and some of them distasteful or sad. And will I find me there?

Chapter 6: The second horizon

26

This is the second horizon. My mother told me that I was a fourth generation Australian. I suppose, having worked out who my parents' siblings were, and I am still questing, that the second horizon is plumbing the scope of my Australian history. What is the end of this? I will be content when I have tracked my family (in its various parts) back to the United Kingdom, which is where I guessed they all came from, including dad's side of the family.

I will be happy to call it quits then. I know I have broadened the horizon, far beyond uncles and aunties, but the new quest makes good sense. And given that there is an existing concept, "the history of my family in Australia", it is not outlandish. Of course, I had a concept of what the answers would be; I was not expecting surprises. They had to be trades people, a succession of them, living in cities, competent and independent, insofar as the market allowed (mum's father had gone broke in the Depression). The men would have wives and families, with several children, they would not own very much, but they would be proud, and they would have a sense of justice. The women would have their place too. They would not simply be faceless females whose presence in the world was encapsulated by "home duties"; they would be workers in their own right, and their medium would be textiles.

There would be no public figures, and at a certain point, the history would fade out.

I need to look at my parents' parents now. I am already well down the track, as I have identified all of the children for both sets of parents (my grandparents – what I call

Generation 2). There are still more comments from my mother that will come up while I am working on my grandparents, and I will keep testing out the truth of those myths. For example, she said that "the Archers looked down on my father because he had married beneath him", that is, by marrying Margaret Florence Mackie. This is an attack on the entire Scottish side of the family. I accept that I am largely English, but I am also one-eighth Scot.

Mum appended the following message to one of her letters: "P.S. Keep searching, you don't know what you may find".

27

I can give the following details about my grandparents. On mum's side we have the following.

Thomas Richard Archer, born 29 November 1886, Pyrmont NSW; died 11 June 1936, Marrickville NSW.

Margaret Florence Mackie, born 18 August 1887, Richmond Victoria; died 20 March 1941, Leichhardt NSW. Married on 1 October 1910 at St David's Church of England, Arncliffe NSW.

These details came easily from the marriage certificate and the two death certificates. It looks tidy and complete, but it presents me with a problem. I had this idea that there would be a few generations of family living in the inner suburbs of Sydney, and then a trip out from England, the migration that would mark the fourth generation back from me.

Yet here I am, in just Generation Two, and it seems that mum's mother was not born in Sydney; she was born in Victoria. Richmond is a suburb of Melbourne. What was the family doing in Melbourne, and why did they come to Sydney? And, you might ask, how did Thomas and Margaret meet?

There is a second pool of questions. Going back to mum's comment about class, are there any indicators that Margaret came from a class "below" Thomas's? We grew up with little money, and little money evident in the surrounding family. All the people we knew in the family (my uncles, aunts and cousins came from inner western suburbs of Sydney, not the suburbs of the "well to do", so I had no reference points for this remark.

What I did have to work with was the occupations stated on the marriage and death certificates. And these did not answer the question. Thomas was a painter (not a creative artist but a tradesperson). He was a painter at the time of his marriage and he was a painter at the time of his death. Moreover, his father, James Archer, was a plasterer, not anything that indicated wealth or high social status. Plasterers and painters, if you were even interested in ranking trades, would have to fall very close to each other.

What of Margaret? Well, her father was a painter. Yes, a painter. At least that suggests the answer to how Thomas and Margaret met. It would make sense if Thomas was apprenticed to George Briggs Mackie. The other thing I noted was that, at the age of twenty-three, when she got married, Margaret had no specified occupation. I have other marriages in this period where the female's occupation is stated as home duties or domestic duties, some where the female is a domestic servant, and just a few where the occupation could be described as genteel. In one case, a "lady", and in another case, "private life".

My theory is that if the woman was from a poor family, she would have an occupation, and it would be either a craft or trade, like dressmaker, or she would be in service, that is, a domestic servant. I am guessing that this Mackie family was not terribly poor. I also have a picture of Margaret Mackie, from mum. Mum says that her mother was about nineteen years old in the photo. She looks very fine, and very finely dressed. So, what am I to do with the myth that the Mackies were beneath the Archers? The only clue is that Thomas Archer was in business; he was not an employee. I am parking this question. Maybe what I discover later will throw light on it.

28

I can give the following details about my dad's parents.

William Thomas Martin, born 19 June 1883, Bethanga, Victoria; died 16 December 1955, Lidcombe State Hospital (usual residence, Annandale NSW).

Elizabeth Hannah Eaglestone, born 4 June 1882, Balmain NSW; died ??? Married on 22 July 1908 at Methodist Church, St Peters NSW.

You can see there is a problem here. I have details of both grandparents' births, I have the details of their marriage, but where is the death of Elizabeth? If I am to believe what is on dad's first marriage certificate, his marriage to Olive Jane Coates on 11 May 1935, Elizabeth Martin was deceased then. Checking the marriage certificate for his second marriage, to mum, on 4 July 1947, seems to confirm this fact.

But I cannot find her death in the BDM records. I tried from 1913, when dad was born, through to 1950. When I started searching for her, I did not know the names of her parents, so I couldn't filter for that. The search yielded seventy-eight records – a lot of people called Elizabeth Martin died in that period. When I restricted the time period to what dad's first marriage certificate asserted (that she was already dead in 1935), the score was twenty-nine records.

Assuming that she died in Sydney did not reduce the score by much; I still had twenty-one records. I decided I couldn't resolve this in my present state of knowledge; there was nothing to distinguish between any of these people, so I put the question aside. But I kept coming back to it.

I worked out her birth date from her marriage certificate – she was twenty-five when she got married, so her birth was around 1882, and she was born in Sydney. I found it in the records and purchased it. Now I was armed with the new knowledge that her middle name was Hannah, and her parents' names were Edward and Helen.

I searched on Elizabeth H. Martin, but neither of the two results had compatible parents' names. I was searching up to 1950 now, trying to be open-minded about what was on the marriage certificates but still convinced that she had died before I was born. Now I looked at the parents' names and there were a couple of suggestive results. One was Elizabeth Hannah – surely this could be Elizabeth Hannah? Her father was Edward, but her mother was Mary Ann, not Helen, and she died at Uralla, on the north coast of New South Wales. This was stretching things a bit.

I was also interested in Harriette Elizabeth – names could get reversed, and the father was Edwin, which was close to Edward. It was in Sydney too, but the mother's name was Ann. Both of these deaths occurred before 1950, which was reassuring, a little. I re-sorted the list, looking at deaths with mother's name equal to Helen, but there was not even one. Then I thought, if Edward could morph into

Edwin, then Helen might morph into Ellen, so I looked up those entries.

One was at Albury, which I was not ready to accept, and the other one, in 1938, had Ralph for a father, and I didn't think Edward would morph into Ralph. I was running out of ideas and finding nothing. Again, I had to leave it and work on other parts of the story, but I was thinking, a person who is married and had seven children does not simply disappear. Among the "wrong person" certificates I accumulated there were some where the death certificate had several sections filled in as "not known", but I couldn't accept that this would be the case for Elizabeth Martin.

As I continued my venture, I found new places to search. I discovered cemeteries. In the family tree on the computer, I was recording the place of burial or cremation as well as the date and place of death, copied from the death certificates. My trip to Woronora Cemetery with one of my sons was the result of my running a report of all the people buried or cremated there. But my next step was to contact the cemeteries to ask them questions. At first I was just asking them to tell me the exact location of particular graves or memorial plaques, but having figured out how they communicate, I started asking them if they had records about certain people, like Elizabeth.

It may seem strange to talk about "how they communicate", but all of the cemeteries talk in different ways. When I was at Woronora, and in the office, it was easy. I just showed the person my list of names and details, and they looked it up on the computer and told me if the person was at the cemetery, and if so, where the grave or memorial was. However, they told me that all this was online and I could search it from home.

Waverley Cemetery was different. There the records were not online, and you had to write them a letter of request, including a cheque for twenty dollars. I was a little dubious about this process, but when the information arrived (there are over twenty graves in this cemetery that contain relatives of mine), it was detailed and it included large (A4) coloured photos of the graves. Rookwood was different again. It is the largest necropolis (defined as a cemetery that is in or near a city, literally "city of the dead") in the southern hemisphere, consisting of 286 hectares and estimated to have received about one million people dead. It has no online search facility (as of 2015).

This is not what its website says, noting that there are several websites pertaining to the cemetery, as it is managed by several different trusts based on religions. The Anglican and General Cemetery Trust that was relevant in Elizabeth's case says on its website that the search facility is "temporarily unavailable". So far, in my experience, it has been unavailable for two years. I thought that perhaps this was evidence of humour among those who have to deal regularly with death.

Nevertheless, you can talk to the people. I rang the office and the lady said that I could ask two questions. This was disconcerting. If I asked for clarification of this statement, would that be one of my two allowed questions? I suspected that I just had to put this niggle aside and push on. I had two questions ready. One was about a person for whom I did know details of their death, which the lady answered for me. The second question was my latest theory – was it possible for someone to be buried at the cemetery without a death certificate? I thought this was a clever thought, what if the Elizabeth's death was simply not in the BDM records?

The lady assured me that this was not possible. To be buried or cremated at the cemetery, a body had to be accompanied by a death certificate. I harboured the subversive thought that there might be an exception to this rule, but certainly it satisfied me that, as a general rule, a person's death has to show up in the BDM records if they died in New South Wales. Of course, there is always another possibility too, that is, that an error has occurred in the BDM records. The first rule of family history searching, I was learning, was actually a question: any (apparent) fact or assumption may be wrong, but which one?

The lady on the phone at Rookwood told me that I could also communicate with them in writing if I had further questions. And yes, I wanted to ask them about Elizabeth Martin. Could they search all their records and tell me if they have persons of this name? Then I would go and look at the graves. However, first I had to eliminate this possibility at Woronora.

28

William Thomas Martin was buried in a grave with his parents, despite having been a husband and father with his own family of six children (not counting the baby that died). It was as if he was going back to his parents because something had gone amiss with his own family. But perhaps Elizabeth Martin was still buried in the cemetery. Perhaps there some shame attached to her, and she was buried somewhere else in the graveyard.

At this stage, mum had not told me about Callan Park. All I knew was that the last evidence of her was when the last child, Frances, was born in September 1920. That, and the assertions on dad's two marriage certificates, in 1935 and 1947, that she was deceased, which I was accepting that I may have to question. So, my next effort was to plan another trip to Woronora.

Beforehand, I looked up the online search facility on the Woronora Cemetery website and wrote a list of all the persons called Elizabeth Martin in the cemetery and their locations.

I had a map of the cemetery from my previous visit, and I marked out all the graves and memorials I had to visit. There were nine of them, spread all over its one hundred and ten acres of trees and gardens and lawns. I started the day as I should, at the café, and I went back there again for lunch. There was an ambience about the place that was beguiling, brewed up out of youth, organic food and inner joy that countered the nearness of death and passing.

I had no high hopes of finding my Elizabeth Martin today, but if I wasn't methodical about this quest, I would end up in hopeless tangles and not know where I was. So I ventured, to one grave after another, up and down the aisles searching for a sequence of numbers that would lead me to the next Elizabeth Martin. I had nine possibilities that ranged from 1941 through to 1980, although the idea of her still being alive while I was growing up was shocking, because I had to think, what are the implications of not knowing you have a grandmother all the time you are growing up? What does that mean in terms of your parents and what they tell you, or worse, what if they did not know?

It took me a few hours to locate all the graves. I had my camera to take pictures of the graves and I wrote down the details on each headstone. I tracked them all down, even if the name wasn't quite right (e.g. Elizabeth Allice Martin) and even if the religion didn't fit with what I knew. Her background was Methodist and Church of England, but I looked up graves where the person was Roman Catholic or Baptist. I had to widen the lens.

None of them was correct. They had husbands, but the husband was not William Thomas Martin. Instead we had Percy, Charles, James George and so on. However, it was fruitful in the sense that I left with the certainty that Elizabeth was not here. William Thomas was here, but she was not.

Now I was ready to write to Rookwood. I told them what I knew about her, and the possible date range of her death. I took the widest range possible, so I asked them to look from 1920 to 1983 (when she would have been one hundred). I wrote my letter in May 2014. I did not get a reply for four months. I had given up. By now there was a growing number of other people who were calling out for my attention, so I was not sitting idly.

In their letter in reply, The Rookwood General Cemetery Trust apologised for the delay. They gave me eight persons, whose deaths ranged from 1921 to 1952. I could have gone on another grave expedition, but I thought the best way to determine if one of these deaths was the right one was to cross-check them with the BDM register. And that did the job. Every one of them could be discounted. For example, Elizabeth Martin, died 22 June 1928 was the wife of James Martin, and looking up their marriage, I could see that she had been Elizabeth Witts.

I appreciated the information. One more wrong fact discounted gets you one step closer to the true story; it helps to make a space where only the truth can fit.

29

During this period of time, I had been gradually filling in other parts of the picture. Two of the people I was finding out about were Elizabeth's parents. And I was learning to look carefully at every piece of information on certificates. Accordingly, I purchased Elizabeth's mother's death certificate. Ellen Eaglestone died in 1937. She is the one who is buried at Woronora

Cemetery with her husband Edwin (yes, Edwin, not Edward, despite Elizabeth's birth certificate), in a double grave with a headstone carved out of sandstone, and Edwin was a stonemason.

This was the piece of information that seemed compelling. The children of the marriage were listed. There was one male, deceased and one female deceased, and two children living: Elizabeth, 56, and Blanche, 52. There are stories about every one of these children, but it was "Elizabeth, living" that captured my attention. If it was true, it meant that Elizabeth was alive in 1937, contrary to what was stated on dad's marriage certificate on 11 May 1935. And if that were the case, she could have been alive in 1947 as well, when dad got married again.

Was the information reliable and accurate? Well, everything on the certificate was filled in, and everything was correct in all the particulars I knew about, such as her husband's name and her parents' names. I was prepared to accept it. This discovery sent me back to the BDM records and I searched after 1947, on the assumption that the assertion about her being deceased on both of dad's marriage certificates was wrong.

Initially this gave me 125 records. That's a lot of Elizabeth Martins in New South Wales. But I added her father's name as Edward and this brought it down to four. I was still uncertain about whether Elizabeth's father's name was Edward or Edwin. The reality was that I had conflicting information on different certificates. None of the records with father equal to Edward was convincing. I did another search with mother equal to Ellen. This gave me three entries, but again, none that were convincing.

There was another possibility. What if one or both of the parents' names were missing? I went looking again. This time there was a record that stood out: Elizabeth Martin who died in 1968 at Parramatta, aged 88 years. Neither parent was named. The age put her birth year as 1880, close enough to be credible. Parramatta was in the general vicinity, a short trip from Rockdale. If this were the case, she did not die until I was eighteen. Again, how could I, or we, not have known?

This was a certificate upon which I waited with some eagerness. I read from the top. It was as per the information in the online index. Then the more specific information: place of death – "Parkview" Private Hospital, Parramatta. I looked at the cause of death – she had had heart disease, many years, and had died of a coronary occlusion, but she had also had mental debility for many years. Was this what happened to dad's mother?

But it was not her. This person had been married to Joseph Martin, her maiden name was Graham, and she had had no children ("no issue"). Interestingly, she had been born at Ballymena in Northern Ireland. Also interesting was the fact that this was one of the people on my list from Rookwood Cemetery, and I cross-checked that list and could see that this was the case.

I was no further ahead. Or was I? What it did reinforce was the idea that even if Elizabeth had a mental illness and was in an institution, she would still have a death certificate.

30

This focus on the difficulty of finding Elizabeth Martin's date of death was mirrored by the difficulty I had in determining the date of her husband's death, although I did resolve it eventually. One of the difficulties of establishing that a record of death is the person you are after is you almost need to know the names of their parents first. You have to take two steps backwards before you can go one step backward. It's an awkward dance.

The problem was that I started out assuming that he had died before 1950, namely, before I was born. And if I were to believe what was on dad's second marriage certificate, he was still alive in 1947. But could I believe the marriage certificate, given what I was finding out about William Thomas Martin's wife? I figured I could, because the situation was not the same, it was the reverse: why would you say someone was alive if they were dead?

At one point I persuaded myself that a William Thomas Martin who died in 1939 could be him, and I bought the certificate. He wasn't the man. His age was close, but he was a council employee who lived at Enmore and who had never married. He was also Roman Catholic, and I knew this was a decisive factor in him being the wrong person. Even when I was a child, that is, post-1950, there was a gulf between Catholics and Protestants in Australian society. They were different tribes; each thought the other was wrong, and wrong in important respects. And occasionally someone might cross the gulf – an intellectual or a lover – but not the average worker.

After that I decided that I needed to be patient, and wait until I had enough surrounding information for the answer to fall out by itself. Part of it was a matter of deciding which data I was going to trust, and I concluded that my William Thomas Martin (yes, I was becoming proprietorial about these new members of my family) had indeed been alive at least as late as 1947.

There was one other death that ached to be considered. A William Thomas Martin had died in 1948, which was perfect – it was between 1947 and 1950. His parents were Thomas and Emma, and he had died at Concord. Concord was close enough to the Rockdale-Arncliffe axis of abode to be worth consideration. The father was Thomas, which fed into the concept of children assuming and carrying on some of the Christian names of their parents.

However, I didn't pursue this possibility. Why? I think I was just absorbing the enormity of the scope of possibilities. There were so many people called Martin, there were even so many people called William Thomas Martin, and if I countenanced that William Thomas Martin might be recorded as William Martin, the possibilities ballooned again. I felt that I should forbear, and wait until I had something more solid: surround the gap until there is a space that only the truth will fit into.

There is a rider to that maxim: even if the truth turns out to be unlikely.

In William Thomas Martin's case, it wasn't that the facts turned out to be unlikely, it was just that I had to absorb the idea that he had not died before I was born. I was five, and I had known nothing about it. I asked my sister, because she had been seven, but she thinks that she hadn't known about it either. She just remembered that visit to the institution and seeing the old bed-ridden person. I don't feel resentment about this, I am just amazed at how different the past was, even this recent past, in my own lifetime. Parents who thought that it was best to say nothing, because I certainly believe that they were told the truth. No, it's even stronger than that – in their understanding they knew that it was best not to tell us kids anything. They knew.

This is so foreign to me. I cannot imagine acting like this with regard to my own children, or even towards my grandchildren, who are still very young. I remember a line from a movie that came out when I was about twenty: "The past is a foreign country; they do things differently there".

In fact, dad's father died a year after we moved to Greenacre. The informant on the death certificate was

Norm Martin, dad's older brother, with whom we had lived for several years.

31

Looking at the death certificate again, I consider "Rank or profession". At his death, dad's father was a "boiler attendant". It sounded rather menial; necessary, perhaps, but relatively unskilled. But hadn't he been called a blacksmith on my father's death certificate? Yes. And on his brother's death certificate, the one who died one day after my father, he was called an iron worker. Was it a question of who was telling the story? Perhaps. On all of my father's various certificates, his father was consistently described as a blacksmith.

On his own marriage certificate, William Thomas Martin was described in the same way: blacksmith. I notice, too, that his father, who was indeed Thomas (so the names do persist in one way or another), was an "engine driver". I did not know how to reconcile all these different job descriptions. I was sure that he was not an *avant garde* career changer. An engine driver – what kind of engine?

I don't have the marriage certificates for all of dad's siblings, but in those that I do have, the blacksmith theme is strong for their father. This part I could understand: my father was not a blacksmith; indeed, none of his brothers were, and this can be understood in terms of the twentieth century and the ascendancy of the motor vehicle. We don't need horseshoes no more. In addition, there was the family's migration to Sydney, which I understood to mean that the children of William Thomas Martin would need to find new occupations. A previous way of living had ended.

The implication of this statement, "a previous way of living had ended", was that there would be a connection between the occupations of William Thomas Martin and his father. What was an "engine driver"? Gradually, incrementally, I gathered pieces of the story together. I think I actually found the death of Thomas Martin before I found the death of William Thomas Martin, that is, I found the father before I found the son. Thomas Martin had come to Sydney too, from Victoria, and he had died in 1945 at Arncliffe. The informant for the certificate was his son, William Thomas Martin.

The death certificate, of course, was full of clues for the next round of stories, but at the moment I was interested in occupations, and his occupation gave another little twist to the developing picture. It said he was an engine driver, but not just an engine driver. He was an engine driver of a kind that I had never heard of: a stationary engine driver. I could see the funny side of this. Here, I had just discovered that my great grandfather was Thomas the Tank Engine, and it seemed that he could only be trusted if the engine was stationary!

Thomas Martin had somehow come to Bethanga in Victoria and spent a significant part of his life there. Bethanga was assuming the proportions of a centre of gravity. A gold-mining town. He had married Phillipa Dower and they had had eleven children, all but one alive at the time of his death. The scope of my modest quest was step by step blowing all of its boundaries. Accordingly, the question of stationary engine drivers was well and truly parked, indefinitely, until one day I was sitting in the tea room at State Records out at Kingswood, waiting for them to retrieve a set of divorce papers. It could have been Norman Martin's, although I have made several trips pursuing divorce papers. I will get to them; they are part of several different strands of the story.

In a state of enforced idleness, I picked up one of the magazines lying on the table, some of which were twenty years old. We see ourselves as being in the present, taking on the role of researcher, looking back at deliberate points in time, yet we are sometimes inhabiting in-between points of time, looking at old magazines that are accidental escapees from the rubbish bin. The magazine dated from the 1990s. It was an issue of *Practical Family History* (UK).

A reader had enquired about the occupation of stationary engine driver. Several readers knew about it. Roy, from Gloucestershire, had a great grandfather, John, who was variously known as an electric engine driver, a driver of machine engines and a tractor engine driver. What this meant was that he operated the engines that produced electricity for the hotel where he was employed. They were, of course, stationary. Anne-Marie, from Norfolk, had a grandfather who was a hydraulic engine driver. The engine he "drove" was a hydraulic pumping or bridge-raising engine related to the docks. Thus, driving meant being an operator of the machinery.

Ian from South Yorkshire had a wife whose grandfather was recorded in a Census as being a stationary engine driver. He worked at a steel works. Ian explained that these engines were in service prior to the common use of electricity. The engines were similar in design to railway steam engines, and the driver was responsible for maintaining a good head of steam and ensuring that a sufficient, continuous supply of power was provided to the machinery. One of the writers said that some of these stationary engines were still in service up until the 1960s (in England).

There was another certificate I had, a marriage certificate of one of Thomas Martin's daughters, where he was described as an engineer. At this point, old memories returned. It was as if someone had tapped me on the shoulder, close, when I wasn't expecting it. I had walked down that path briefly, just after I left school, at seventeen. Glenn Martin, engineer. I hadn't really wanted to go down that path at all, but I hadn't known what else to do, and it seemed a sensible, and attainable, thing to do. Now it seems that my grandfather had been some kind of engineer. Was it in my blood? Was that why, in my dearth of ideas about what to do with my life, I had chosen engineering instead of something else – teacher, surveyor, businessman, lawyer, journalist, philosopher, academic?

We live in an age of lazy scepticism, so people tend to be dismissive of such ideas, but of course, they have no ideas of their own, and no credible rebuttal of the ideas that landed in my brain of their own accord. It's just easier to say you believe in nothing, although, at the same time, people are prepared to accept the next big proposition about neuroscience or the origin of the universe.

At the end of high school I enrolled in a civil engineering degree, and I worked at it studiously for two whole years. Although I passed my exams it was hard work. It was not enjoyable. Looking around didn't help, because no one else seemed to be enjoying it either. The other students just seemed to think that this was how things were, and I could see that they would spend the rest of their lives doing that, and so would I. One of the first brave decisions of my life was to leave the engineering course.

In one sense, it wasn't a real decision. I just decided that I couldn't continue along a path that I was going to hate for forty years. But I didn't know what else to do, and the easiest course was to follow what you could imagine to be fate, and switch to teaching. Accordingly, I finished tertiary studies and became a school teacher, teaching mathematics. To most people around me, and certainly to family (principally, my mother), this looked like success and achievement. That was a trap that took me nearly fifteen years to emerge from.

Thomas Martin, you shocked me. I have always been committed to following my own course, but for so many years I didn't have any clue as to what that might be. You make me think there is some weight in history, and if we really want to find our own path, we have to know our own past, which is to say, our family, and make our choices in the light of that. And in some cases, we may have to stand against our family's past. And of course, our family (all the generations of it) needs us to do that. We have only two choices for our lives: replicate or innovate. To replicate is to die (often slowly, imperceptibly); to innovate is to live, and to live is to reinvigorate the family tree.

There is no destiny. Well, there is, unless you decide that there doesn't have to be. Innovate or replicate.

I still don't know what this business is about stationary engines.

Chapter 7: Where do occupations come from?

32

I am eager to pursue the Martin family down into Victoria, but there is another person still waiting for an explanation of his occupation – my father, the painter. What mum told me was that when she met dad, he was a storeman; he didn't have a trade. And it was through her family that dad acquired a trade as a painter. They helped him, and he studied a course in painting and he started to make his way in the trade. Now I have to see how this matches up against the records I have acquired.

There are a few strands to the story. When dad got married in 1935, his occupation was "storeman". When he married mum in 1947, he was a painter. I wonder how this fits into the history of the Martin family across these years. The picture I have formed of father William Thomas was that he worked as a blacksmith, or some kind of ironworker, in an engineering firm around Rockdale. I suspect that dad and his brothers worked there at some stage too.

It may be that the reality is much stronger than this. In other words, maybe father William Thomas actually owned, or part-owned, the firm. Maybe he, or his father Thomas, had even started it when they came to Sydney. This thought did not come to me until I went through all of dad's siblings and realised that they could have all worked in the same place. Dad was a storeman; so was his brother George. Dad's brother Norm was a millhand; so was brother William Thomas.

I admit that I did not think of this possibility because I carried over mum's attitudes towards the mill where she had first worked to the place where the Martins worked. I carried this idea that the workplace was not a pleasant place, and everyone just wanted to get out of it. But maybe this was not the case. If I allow myself the assumption that the Martins – dad's father and dad and his brothers – worked at the same place, an engineering firm, and that the firm may have been owned by the family, then it all takes on a very different complexion.

Now there is the possibility that it is a family business, productive and commercially successful. It also suggests a family history where members of the family worked together in the same business. I am glimpsing, perhaps, into a deeper past.

But my father became a painter. Was there a disruption in the engineering business? Did it atrophy, and my father had to get out? At first I thought of the Great Depression. Dad was born in December 1913, so he was about sixteen when the Wall Street stock market crashed, with reverberations around the world. The family business could have disintegrated. But the facts don't fit. It is in 1935 that dad is working as a storeman.

It is what happened before then that is interesting. Mum told me that dad had left home when he was quite young. He would have been living with Uncle Paul and Aunty Maud. I asked mum what age that was, and she said he was about fourteen or fifteen. She said he had wanted to work on a farm, and he did. He left Sydney and found a family farm up on the Hawkesbury north of Sydney and he lived and worked there for a while. But it was the Depression that put an end to that. The family said they couldn't afford to keep him on, and he ended up coming back to Sydney.

But now I had to take into account something else mum had told me, and it dates from 1951. In 1951 there was a severe recession, and dad was put off from work because there was a downturn in the company he worked for, Pilkington Glass. The circumstances were remembered because dad had worked there for nineteen years, and the company refused to pay him his long service leave. At that time, you did not become eligible for long service leave until you had been employed for fifteen years.

Mum said that dad had worked in two different departments over the time he had been there, so the company was arguing that dad's service had not been continuous. I imagine the company's bookkeeper saying to the manager that the company had an opportunity to save some money here. No hard feelings, it's just that business is business. And those workers, they just try and turn everything into a moral issue. Surely they can understand that business is tough, and companies have to make savings wherever they can.

And when the union took the company to court and won dad's case, after many months, I suppose they reacted by saying that the court was arguing on a technicality. My father had a strong sense of justice. It was only a couple of years later when the incident with the real estate agent occurred and again he had to resort to the courts. In his next job, at the gas works, where he worked as a painter until he died, dad was the shop steward for the union. There are people who would brand this as radical, but he was simply doing his bit to ensure that people who were not in positions of power could not be brutalised or cheated by those who did hold power.

At the gas works, occasionally someone would ask dad to do a painting job for them on the weekends. This was useful, because mum and dad were trying to pay off the house and carry out improvements. There was a manager who asked dad to do a job at his house, and dad did it, he even fronted up the money for the paint. Then the manager didn't pay him. My gentle and mild-mannered father went to the manager and told him, "If you don't pay me that money you owe me this week, everyone in this company will know what kind of a person you are." He got the money.

There were other managers that dad had respect for, who treated people fairly and decently, and dad did painting jobs for them without any problems at all. There was mutual respect. It's the philosophy that you can do anything you like if you can justify it as "business" that I despise. Someone can work for you for nineteen years, but it's okay to cheat them out of their long service leave because it saves the company a few dollars. And of course, we know the same does not apply to executives when they leave; they get golden handshakes.

It's like that kid who says "I should have all the lollies". The kid has got no reason at all, he (and she) just has unabashed gall, but they would love it if you were foolish enough to believe them.

33

I am back to doing arithmetic now. Tracking back nineteen years from 1951 takes us to 1932. Dad starts work at Pilkington Glass as a storeman, but sometime before 1947 he becomes a painter. That must explain the two different departments he worked in. The only thing I am not clear about was how this transition occurred. Dad's first wife died in 1943 and dad and mum got together after that. But they must have already known each other, because dad's sister had married mum's brother in 1941. Dad was ten years older than mum, and when Thelma got married to Victor, dad and Olive had one child, James.

However, I am sorry to say I can get no further with this. The reality was that mum's father had died in 1936, and as far as I know there was no one else in the family (the Archers) who carried on the painting trade. I don't know what mum's story means; I have just had to let some things go.

But this theme of occupations is an important theme. It is a central part of the family story. I am not interested in accumulating a book of names, places and dates that is not much different to a telephone directory. There is a story here (yes, of course, many stories), about the dynamics of people and the families they inhabit and create, that I want to understand.

I think it is best to park the question of occupations now and return to it later. I am interested in what happens to occupations over a longer period of time, several generations, and how it changes over time and from place to place. I need to keep on the track of pushing back to the next generation, and then the next.

34

Generation Two is my grandparents – on dad's side, William Thomas Martin and Elizabeth Eaglestone; on mum's side, Thomas Richard Archer and Margaret Florence Mackie. About the detail of their lives I do not know a lot. For example, I do not even have a photo of William Thomas Martin. But I also felt that I would come to understand more about them if I found out about their parents. It sounds like a truism: to know the children, you have to know the parents.

In any case, it's difficult to find out about a person without finding something out about their parents. Your parents appear on your birth certificate, your marriage certificate and your death certificate, even their occupation.

Accordingly, I am now looking at Generation Three, my great grandparents. Already there are questions about them, such as the question of geography. I have noted that on mum's side, her mother, Margaret Florence Mackie, was born in Victoria (Richmond, in Melbourne) and on dad's side, his father, William Thomas Martin, was also born in Victoria, at Bethanga. I thought it was curious that both families hailed from Victoria yet it seemed clear enough that they had not met until after they arrived in Sydney (and I still think my father was called Sydney because the family came to the city of that name, and it was a significant event for them).

On dad's side I had nothing now except what the records told me. There were no stories from dad. I don't ever remember dad talking about his family, or anything about his life growing up. It was from mum, and only recently, that I learned that Aunty Maud (with Uncle Paul) brought him up. I still had some stories from mum that I hadn't got to yet, because they were stories about Generation Two and Generation Three. I was working my way steadily backwards, and I was keen to get to them, but there is not a lot of leap-frogging in this work.

It was interesting the stories I didn't have too. Mum remembers her mother, but I have never heard her speak about her mother being born in Victoria. I wonder if she knew. I keep comparing it with what I knew about my own parents growing up. We did know that mum and dad were born in the inner suburbs of Sydney. I guess the idea of geography was in the air because we moved house when we children were young and maybe we wondered where our parents had moved from prior to that. But it was part of mum's memory – "When your father and I got married we rented a room in Mrs Marsh's house at Drummoyne, and after Helen was born in 1948 we had to think about getting somewhere more substantial, and it was difficult because it was after the war and there was nothing around to rent, and then the breakdown happened with Norm and his wife, and Frances (mum's sister) suggested that we could work something out with him and help each other."

With my own children, geography is part of family lore as well. The geography is in their birth dates. Elvina was born in Sydney before we left, Holly was born in Mackay in Queensland, but the twins, timothy and Andrew, were born in Horseshoe Creek at Kyogle, and Rohan was also born there. Now I am back in Sydney, but the trail tells a tale.

It seems that I am on the trail to Victoria. I had got used to searching the BDM records in New South Wales, but I had to start again in Victoria. I had to search for the registry itself first. It operated differently from the New South Wales registry, but I learned its methods. Essentially, it was there and it worked, and I would get used to it. It was back to the essential question of whether I had the right information to feed into it, and whether the records would prove to exist or not. I was always ready for the trail to simply fade out, and I didn't know how soon that would occur.

35

I wondered if my parents, unlike myself and my siblings, had had grandparents alive during their childhood. It goes like this: on my mum's father's side, both of his parents had died before mum was born. But on her mother's side, her father died when she was three, so that would have been only a faint memory if anything at all. But my mum's grandmother lived until mum was eleven. However, she died in the State Hospital at Auburn, and I think she had been there for some time. The informant on the death certificate was the manager of the hospital, not a family member. At the time, mum's father and mother were both alive. The chances are that there was not much contact between my mum and her family, and perhaps mum did not even know about her.

On my dad's side? On his father's side, both the parents were alive during my dad's lifetime. Dad's grandfather Thomas did not die until dad was thirty-two; he lived until he was eighty-nine – a good innings, as they say. Dad's grandmother died when dad was nineteen. Did dad know them? Surely he did. They lived down the road at Arncliffe, because I think dad grew up at Rockdale, and the mental picture I have of Thomas and his wife is that they were like patriarch and matriarch of the Martin host in Sydney, well-established financially and a stable force for their descendants.

As to dad's grandparents on his mother's side, his mother's father died when dad was only three (Eaglestone), but the wife lived until dad was twenty-four, and again, I am sure that dad knew her. This is not to say that there was much contact between them, but I know that the mother and daughter (dad's mother) kept in touch. So for dad, we have this picture that three of his four grandparents were alive all through his childhood and he probably knew them.

Then again, we children never heard anything about our dad's childhood. It was an area of silence. You could say that as children we were thrust towards the future and there was no past. We were thrust towards achievement as a new start, but a new start from what? It was as if everything in the past had been annihilated, and what we had was that stark block of land at Greenacre.

When we moved into the temporary dwelling at Greenacre in 1954, it was a big block of land that was mostly covered with scrappy bush. Yes, even as a child who had grown up in a dense suburb with houses all around, just two doors up from the busy Canterbury Road at Wiley Park, I thought the bush at Greenacre was scrappy. There was one large ironbark tree next door, and over the road there was a stand of eucalypts about fifty metres away. It was difficult to see the road from our dwelling because of the bush, and the bush stood there for a couple of years before it was cleared.

It took five slow years for the new house to be built. Most of that time was spent with mum and dad working on sorting out money and a builder. In the end they got help from the Housing Commission, which was trying to be innovative in getting people into their own homes. The house took about six months to build. In those days, builders did not surround construction sites with protective fences, and as children we played among the foundations and on the wooden frames as they rose from the brick piers.

Of course, we weren't supposed to play there. Mum told us not to, and the builders didn't like it, but they couldn't watch us all the time, and we didn't do any harm.

The house was a symbol of building a future from nothing. There was just scrappy bush to start with, then it was cleared, with the smell of cut timber and cut grass, and then men came with mattocks, string and stakes to mark out the foundations, and then came a truck loaded with bricks that were unloaded by hand, and then there was a cement mixer. After months of building, the house was finished, and was painted glossy white, offsetting the green tiles on the roof. It was modest, but it was neat, it fulfilled the purpose, and it was what our parents were achieving by themselves alone, without the backing of the family as institution.

This was how it was, and we did not know otherwise, although we did have that general sense that there were other families in society who "got a start" from their parents or their extended family who had money. But that was okay, because there were lots of poor people around too, who weren't managing to do what our parents were doing; our family was managing to inch its way forward to security, to a house of its own.

It was the other lack that was less tangible at the time, but somehow more telling when looking back on it. It was the lack of family as cheer squad, as older people who are there to celebrate your milestones. For mum, it was a couple of sisters who felt gladness for her when we moved into the new house. For dad, it was Norm, but then Norm was immersed in the break-up of his first marriage, and then finding a new lady to share his life with. That seemed to be the extent of the family as a living institution for us.

The future was a place that quivered with social opportunity and trepidation, but the past was another country. And like the countries behind the Iron Curtain when we were growing up, the past was walled off.

36

Apart from the health issues of mum's parents, and what my sister had said about dad's father's health, I still did not have any feeling for my grandparents – their situation, the kind of work they did, whether they had stable families, whether they were skilled, whether they had dignity. I wasn't really expecting to find out if they were happy or sad. But I would find out what I could. Now I just wanted to learn what I could.

Do I need any further explanation than this? I have heard the word "hobby" used in reference to people who pursue family history. I do not have hobbies, and this quest is not a hobby. Hobbies, in my mind, are for people who are either bored with their lives or who are escaping from their lives. I am not bored and I am not escaping. I am plunging in; I am trying to understand.

I may be a creature of my time. I was eighteen when students around the world revolted and rioted, questioning and challenging everything. I was coloured by that, even if I wasn't a blind and crazed revolutionary. The revolution was inside me too. Something was blasting its way out.

Years later the Iron Curtain came down, and we discovered that there were people on the other side of it, people just like us, but shaped differently by the experiences they had had. The curtain drawn against my family's past is coming down now. I know there are people there, who have a relationship to me. I may not be the same as them, but I have come from them; I am part of their story, and I wish to know it, and stand in appreciation of their experience, even as I make my own way.

I am conscious, too, that things tend to occur at the appropriate time, so I am not regretting not having done this earlier. I was charged by the occasion of my mother's ninetieth birthday, peeved by the fact that I knew so little of my family. Of mum's family I knew just the stories mum had told us, and they were scanty, and of dad's family I knew practically nothing. But if I had tried this any earlier, there would have been no internet, and the whole project would have been gruellingly hard.

Even during the two years I have been working on this project, the avenues have opened up, by the month, even by the week. For example, I could not get a fix on dad's mother's grandparents until one month I learned that a new search engine had been released for Tasmanian records. Suddenly I had breakthroughs, several astonishing breakthroughs.

However, the information has, for the most part, come slowly, piece by piece, incrementally. With Generation Three (my great grandparents) I was so very ignorant. On dad's father's side, I found the death of my great grandmother first. Phillipa Martin died in Sydney in 1931 at the age of seventy-two years, another good innings. I saw that she had been born in South Australia, but married in Bethanga, Victoria at the age of twenty-one. Her father was a miner.

A miner's family had come from South Australia to Victoria and their daughter had married another miner. I was learning that mining was a strong theme in my father's family, but that still didn't mean much to me. At the moment I was just trying to stake out the territory by finding births, deaths and marriages. I figured that putting my family into a social context was a later project.

I knew so little about Phillipa and Thomas Martin that in my notes I wrote: "Lots of missing information (father's and mother's names). Numerous possibilities in Victoria. Phillipa died in Sydney in 1931. Did she come to Sydney when her husband died? Where are the children? Did they marry in Victoria?"

In the end it was the cemetery at Woronora that helped to fill the space. Thomas Martin was buried with his wife. That was where I learned that Thomas had lived to be eighty-nine, so his birth date was back in 1856. That was a shivery moment, realising that I was back in the middle of the previous century from when I was born. That was when I started thinking about social context in earnest. This was before the federation of Australia in 1901. It was another door opening into mystery.

When I got Thomas's death certificate, the picture started to fill out. There had been eleven children. Indeed, this had been on Phillipa's death certificate too, but there was only so much I could take in at once, and as well as this, I wanted the confirmation of details from the second certificate. But the details checked out – the names and ages of the children corresponded, and the names, dates and locations of the marriage with Thomas fitted. It all seemed reliable.

One detail I wasn't ready for – Thomas's date and place of birth. His death certificate said he was born at St Ives, Cornwall. He died at eighty-nine, but he had been in Australia for eighty-eight years. This meant that, with respect to him, I was a third-generation Australian, taking this to mean I am the third generation born in Australia. Mum had said she thought dad's family had come to Australia in the same generation as her family, which would make me third-generation Australian-born on both mum's and dad's sides.

This was showing me the muddiness of these concepts. Everyone has eight grandparents, and the answer could be different with respect to each one of them. Even for this one couple, Thomas and Phillipa, the answer was different, because Phillipa was born in Australia, at Kooringa in South Australia. With respect to her I am at least a fourth-generation Australian. And as yet I had no idea about mum's side of the family.

The other aspect I was picking up was about movement, or migration. Families had moved, and it is fair to assume that there was purpose in this movement. Phillipa's family had moved from South Australia to Victoria, to a tiny town in the north of Victoria where she had married Thomas. Later (how much later? I didn't know where the children had been born yet) they had moved to Sydney. And Thomas had come to Australia from Cornwall at the age of one. I have to say, my imagination and my curiosity were stirred.

I noticed the names of the children too. Here were names I had seen before. There were Frances and William. It seemed that William, dad's father's name, had a lineage of its own, and Frances, the youngest child of William Thomas Martin and Elizabeth Eaglestone, may have been named after her aunty. I didn't know what the reasons were for parents naming their children, but it was happening, and it was not accidental. I didn't know if this was a Cornwall thing, or a generally English thing to do, or if it extended to Scotland as well. (I knew I was going to get to Scotland sooner or later; I had the Mackie line yet to follow from my mother's side.)

I was excited, but anxious too. If I was going to continue, I would have to learn how to search records in Britain, and apart from Aunty Dollie's great expedition in the pre-internet days, I had no idea how to go about this. I was also wary about internet subscription services. The promises seemed so ludicrous – just enter a name and you will instantly find your entire family tree! I somewhat doubted that, and I knew already from my searches in New South Wales, especially with common names like Martin and Archer, that you could search for a birth, even narrowed down to ten years or less, and find thirty or more possibilities, with nothing to choose between them.

The crunch was, if you wanted to be sure, the essential thing to do was to buy certificates, and I already had a growing pile of "wrong persons". You couldn't seriously approach this kind of project by buying every one of the thirty possible certificates. Well, if you had an unlimited budget, I suppose you could, but the more elegant and professional way to proceed was by trying another way to narrow the field, to narrow it so much that only the truth could fall out of that space. I admit that I was watching police detective shows on television now with a new eye. I was interested in how the detectives thought. I asked, what would they do in this situation? How would they go about it? What would they notice?

37

At this point I can give the following details about my dad's dad's parents. This is the first of four sets of great grandparents. This is the one that starts to open up my father's side of the family. It goes back to Cornwall in the far west of England, and it seems to involve mining. How would I have guessed that from what I knew of my father growing up? Only from one thing – he was short and stocky, and he had thick, wiry, black hair that there was no point in combing; he just brushed it straight back.

My sister has the same hair, although hers is blonde. I always thought the thick, wiry hair was a puzzle. Where had it come from? For myself, my characteristic is that I am short and stocky like dad was, and so is one of my sons, Rohan. I don't know about the hair, but short and stocky for miners seems to fit. One day Rohan came around to my house. The previous week I had been sharing these new discoveries about our family with him, and my wonder about it all.

I was outside, hanging wet clothes on the line, and he said, straight away after saying hello, "I know why you and I are short and stocky. It's those Cornish miners. Generations of them had been mining, and their bodies came to suit their work, down in those tunnels and shafts. It helps to be short when you are doing that kind of work." What struck me was that he had taken in this new knowledge and understood it in an embodied way – his very body spoke about his ancestry. Wonderful.

I am not taking any of this too seriously. I am sure that not all people from Cornwall are short and stocky, but there is a thread of story in all this, and not just a thread of story. The truth is indeed in our bodies. I am learning that I am, in fact, genetically connected to people who go back to that part of the world. One (or more) of them came to Australia, for some reason, and their descendants ended up in Sydney, in those inner suburbs, and the thread, both in story and in blood, comes down to me.

Thomas Martin, born 1856, St Ives, Cornwall; died 27 December 1945, 79 Station Street, Arncliffe NSW.

Phillipa Dower, born 30 October 1857, Kooringa, Burra, South Australia; died 12 January 1931, 79 Station Street, Arncliffe NSW. Married on 18 January 1879 at Bethanga, Victoria.

This information is not quite complete. At this stage, I had yet to delve into English, or Cornish, records to find the record of Thomas's birth. I noticed on the death certificate for this Thomas Martin that while he may have been born in Cornwall, he had spent eighty-eight of his eighty-nine years in Australia, so he had come out to Australia when he was a baby. Perhaps that was why mum had the idea, presumably from dad, that this Thomas had been one of the first generation to be born in Australia.

[About three months after finishing writing this part, I had initiated myself into English records, and the Cornwall database as well. But I still couldn't find a record for Thomas Martin's birth that was convincing. Either the record in question was not the right town or the date wasn't quite right. But my delving had unearthed the fact that the surname in previous generations was sometimes "Martins" rather than "Martin". So, I tried again using "Martins" and I found the record straight away: 13 May 1856, at Street-An-

Garrow, St Ives, Cornwall. Once they were in Australia, the Martin family dropped the 's'. New world, new start, new name.]

Thomas had lived so long that it is not surprising the family may have simply thought he was born in Australia. After the myth about "people in the family" dying before they reached fifty, Thomas was an impressive statistic to the contrary. I came across a discussion of the Book of Job, in the Old Testament, which quoted these lines:

In ripe age you shall go to the grave,
Like a wheat sheaf stacked in due season.

One hopes that it was like that for Thomas.

Gradually I dabbled in the Victorian registry of BDM, not confidently, but just trying to build step by step. I found the record of marriage of Thomas Martin and Phillipa Dower. Thomas was twenty-two and Phillipa was twenty-one. Thomas's profession is stated to be "Miner", while Phillipa has "No profession". As to their parents' professions, Thomas's father is an engineer, and Phillpa's father is a miner. The unifying theme is clear – both families are mining families, and there is lineage involved. The new question is this: how far back does mining go in both families?

I say "both families" because I was keenly aware that in terms of blood, the female and male lines of the family are just as important as the other. My name might be Martin, but from my grandparents' generation, there are four family names that abide in my blood – Eaglestone, Archer and Mackie just as much as Martin. In my great grandparents' generation there are seven family names besides Martin. I wondered how many family names I would discover. Thinking this made me feel closer to other people; the world was rapidly filling up with people I was related to.

The marriage of Thomas and Phillipa was conducted according to the rites of the Wesleyan Church. This was something else that hovered at the fringes of my knowledge. I was brought up in the Church of England, before it went modern and called itself the Anglican Church in Australia. I learned a little bit about the history of Protestantism, how, after King Henry VIII broke away from Rome, there had been various movements where groups had broken away from the Church of England. There were the Presbyterians, the Methodists and the Congregationalists.

John Wesley was the instigator of the Methodists, but after a while another splinter formed, of people who thought that their church was not being true to the founding principles. And so the Wesleyan Methodists were born, and this group was strong in Cornwall. You see I am a rudimentary church historian, but what is washing around me is multiplying layers of social history. My family is an expression, not just of girl-meets-boy, repeated many times, but of the social history of the time.

Do I think this is a bit thin as a picture of social history? Well, how about this? I ask, where was the marriage held? The safest answer, of course, is in a church, and to be more precise, a Wesleyan church. But the ceremony was not held in a church at all. It was held in the private residence of William Dower, the father of the bride (I am reading from the marriage record). So now I want to know all about Bethanga and what was happening there at the time.

Chapter 8: Bethanga, Victoria

38

As we know, this Thomas Martin at some point migrated to Sydney and ended his days there. (I keep saying "this Thomas Martin" because his father was called Thomas as well. I briefly toyed with the idea of using "Thomas Senior" and Thomas Junior", but I rejected it for two reasons. First, I find it a little inappropriate to refer to someone who lived to be eighty-nine as Junior. And second, I guessed that there would be other ancestors in the Martin family who would also be called Thomas, so what would be the sense of Senior and Junior when there were more than two generations of them?

Similarly, the idea of Thomas Martin I and Thomas Martin II struck me as being pompous and ridiculous. I can only see that as being used by a rich industrialist who has founded a dynasty and is fabulously wealthy, or someone who has a title under the realm. Clearly neither of those possibilities fits. My family were apparently skilled professionals, but not capitalist entrepreneurs or nobility. And lastly, the family itself has shown no sign of indulging in such airs. Yes, that is more than two reasons.

Bethanga in 1879 was a primitive settlement but it was seized with the excitement of gold. Gold had been reported in the area as early as 1852, and there were alluvial gold fields along several creeks around the small town. What made a difference was that on New Year's Day, 1876, someone discovered gold in a quartz reef. There was also copper in the area. This was a different proposition. While the pursuit of gold on the surface, in creeks, was generally the province of small-scale speculators (and let's admit, that was occasionally wildly successful), the retrieval of gold from reefs was a serious enterprise that required investment, machinery and expertise.

Firstly, the gold was underground, and required the expertise of miners who could build shafts. And secondly, the gold had to be extracted from quartz, and this was a process that, again, required expertise and investment. Instead of lone operators and small collectives setting up sluices in creeks, this enterprise involved investors who could be persuaded that there would be an appropriate level of sustained returns, and managers, engineers and employees.

Going back to the marriage of Thomas and Phillipa, they got married in a town that was getting underway as a mining centre. The post office opened in 1876, and the Great Eastern Copper Smelting Works started operations in 1878, but the town was not well-enough established to have churches, much less a church for a small protestant denomination. Hence, the father of the bride, William Dower, offered his house for the wedding.

They did manage to procure the services of a Wesleyan minister for the occasion, a fact of wonder in itself. Where did he come from? His name was Thomas Angwin. I suspect that he was from Cornwall. In fact, I suspect that there was a small multitude of skilled miners from Cornwall in Victoria at the time, so of course there would be a minister to tend to them, as ministers did. Currently, there is even a website devoted to the miners of Cornwall who migrated to Australia.

Once again, it seems that I can only tell the story of the person by telling the story of their parents. It wasn't this Thomas who chose to come to Australia, it was his parents, Thomas and Mary Ann Martin.

39

I want to focus on Thomas Martin the Younger, because the big question of his life (for me) is why and how he came to Sydney. But at the same time I am being drawn into the story of Thomas Martin the Elder. (You see, I have invented assignations for them anyway.)

Before I go there, let me say who the children of Thomas and Phillipa are. The young Phillipa, over a period of twenty-one years, had eleven children. Their names are: Mary Ann, Frances Matilda, William Thomas, Martha, Thomas, Elizabeth, Stella May, Norman, Paul, Olive Myrtle, Egbert Albert (Yes, I have mentioned him before, when I was looking for someone to look after my father in 1920). The names that may be familiar from this list are William Thomas (he is my grandfather), Paul – the one who looked after my father while he was growing up, and Stella May – it looks as if she was the one that may have looked after one of my dad's younger sisters, Thelma and Frances.

You might ask, were all of these children born in Bethanga, and what happened to them? Indeed, in the end I discovered that all of the children were born in Bethanga. Egbert was born in 1900. But what is interesting is that some of the children came to Sydney, and some didn't. Some of them made their lives in Bethanga, or thereabouts. They married someone local, they joined the Bethanga Australian Rules Football Club; they had children in the area.

The crunch for me was when I went out to State Records at Kingswood and got access to the probate of Thomas Martin's will (1946). I figured that Thomas had lived in Sydney for a long time, and his life was here. Yet, when I looked at the probate package, the two executors of the will were both from Bethanga, not Sydney. They were a son and a son-in-law.

You trust executors. They are your remaining link with this life when you are gone. They express and effect your last wishes. And (this) Thomas Martin's will named as executors two people who belonged to his old life in Bethanga. That fact spoke to me immensely of my own bond with a former life. I lived in Horseshoe Creek, Kyogle for nineteen years, and I have been back in Sydney now for almost the same length of time, but if someone were to say to me suddenly, "Where is the place you call home?" I would say Horseshoe Creek.

So I felt a huge bond with Thomas at that moment. "Home" is where the most significant things in your life happened. I had thought, naively, always naively, that Thomas had come to Sydney and that was all there was to it. The old life was gone. I understood it pragmatically. The gold had run out, and that style of life had run its course. The future was in the big city, and for some reason Sydney had been more of an attraction than Melbourne. But, as my own experience showed, pragmatic reasons do not account for all that is in the heart.

At the age of eighty-nine, Thomas's will expressed his lasting, inexorable bond with Bethanga.

Thomas may have been the child. It may have been his father (Thomas the Elder) who made the lasting impact on the community of Bethanga. But Thomas the Younger did not disappoint. He picked up the Martin baton as an expert in mining, the descendant of a long line of miners, and became the manager of the Lady Rose goldmine at nearby Chiltern.

I can see how this taps into economic history as a phase and a development. First there is the wildness of speculation, of thousands of people turning up in Australia because there is the chance of instant riches. But then there is a second phase, that belongs to the planners. These are the people who raise capital and garner expertise to pursue and create an enterprise. They are methodical, and the goal is not instant riches, but a stream of revenue.

However, despite the methodical mindset and the planning, the second-wave capitalists are not assured of success, despite the hope encapsulated in the raising of capital. They are still reliant on the actuality of what is hidden in the earth. And the truth was, the Lady Rose mine petered out. It operated from 1909 to 1915 – just a few years.

The Chiltern area was ridden with high hopes in the 1860s. It was heralded as "the new Ballarat" and a newspaper was started. Perhaps those two facts are not disconnected. The Lady Rose mine started as a capital-raising venture in about 1908, just outside of Chiltern, to mine and extract gold and tungsten. The money was used to sink a shaft, purchase machinery, and build a manager's house and explosives magazine.

The mine did not fulfil its promise. The ore was not obtained in sufficient quantity. The close of the Lady Rose mine was followed by the closure of other mines in the Chiltern area. The current population of Chiltern is about one thousand, in contrast to Ballarat's ninety-five thousand.

It seems clear enough that the decline of mining in the Chiltern and Bethanga areas was what precipitated the Martin family move to Sydney, sometime in the early 1900s.

I see this as a radical move from the perspective of what I know now. It was the end of a long tradition of mining for the Martin family. Who knows how long? Hundreds of years, or perhaps even thousands?

When Phillipa died, in 1931, a notice appeared in what I think was a local paper in Chiltern. It said:

The death occurred at Arncliffe (NSW) on 12th January, of a well-known district personage, Mrs Phillippa Martin, wife of Mr Thomas Martin. Deceased was a native of Bethanga, her maiden name being Dower. For some time she resided at Chiltern, her husband being the manager of the Lady Rose mine. Mrs Thomas Skerry, of Chiltern, is a daughter.

Phillipa was not simply an ordinary person in the Bethanga and district community; she was a "personage". If I say that this is a tribute to her father-in-law, you will understand soon.

40

Something happened in Cornwall that brought Thomas Martin to Australia. I am not talking about Phillipa's husband; I am talking about Thomas's father. I think there was push and pull involved, and probably advertising too. The pull was the pull of expert miners to Australia occasioned by the advent of deep underground mining. Copper had been discovered in South Australia, and miners from Cornwall were being actively enticed to the colonies to set up shafts and operate machinery. Thomas the Elder was an 'engineer', which is to say, an operator of machinery.

I learned that there was a push effect as well. Tin mining had been an economic activity in Cornwall for over two thousand years, but in the mind-nineteenth century, as the British Empire expanded, cheaper tin was being obtained from the Far East, so that many thousands of the tin miners of Cornwall were, to use a modern phrase, thrown out of work. So it was not just the attraction of the Australian colonies that was at play; it was also that their traditional occupation at home was drying up.

I see the enormity of this. Tin mining in Cornwall had been a way of life for longer than memory trails into the past. Tin is a component of bronze, and it is said that tin mining in Cornwall began earlier than 2000 BC. Cornwall was part of trade across Europe and the Middle East during the Roman Empire. One legend has it that Cornish tin was incorporated in the brass work in King Solomon's temple. Another legend is that Jesus came to Cornwall as a youth with his uncle, Joseph of Arimathea, who was a merchant.

I see that tin mining was a long-time way of life, one that was tough and dangerous, working underground with only candles for light, and having to contend with the threat of water and cave-ins many hundreds of feet underground. But over long periods of time, people develop a sense of harmony with the vicissitudes of the enterprise, a spirit develops about the work, and a camaraderie develops, with notions of expertise and distribution of responsibilities among the community.

Moreover, mining was not just the work of men. Women and children were also involved. The women carried out many of the jobs on the surface, processing the ore that the men brought up from below. They were called 'bal maidens', the word 'bal' coming from the Cornish language and meaning 'a mine'.

Children had jobs fetching and carrying. I am not romanticising this, but I think there is, nevertheless, a powerful communal spirit that arises when a whole community works together in this way. From a Marxist perspective, it may all be simply exploitation, but there are things you see when you look from other perspectives. There is singing and cheerfulness that would be inexplicable. There is the interest in finding new ways to carry out tasks – the mind of the engineer. And there is the mysterious overlay of a people who have their own different language. I feel as if I have stumbled into a village that I used to belong to, but I do not even know how to talk to the people.

In the nineteenth century, this long-time way of life saw the acceleration of change. Tin mining benefited from Sir Humphry Davy's miner's lamp and the advent of machinery to pump out the water, but at the same time it became subject to economic vagaries, which were sometimes catastrophic.

Whatever the particular background or the nature of the decision was, Thomas Martin the Elder got on a ship with his young family at Plymouth in April 1857 to head out to Australia. The ship was the *Carnatic*, and they were heading for Adelaide, South Australia. I thought that the final destination was Burra, one hundred miles north of Adelaide. Copper had been discovered there in the late 1840s, and miners from Cornwall had already made the journey to be part of the new venture, and to take the chance for a new life. Later, I discovered that Thomas had not gone to Burra; he had started up a venture of quite a different kind.

Among the early Cornish adventurers at Burra were William and Elizabeth Dower, whose child, Phillipa, was later to marry Thomas the Younger, in Bethanga.

At the time of embarking from Plymouth, Thomas Martin was just twenty-three. His wife Mary Ann (born Mary Ann Williams), was a couple of years older. They had one child, Thomas, who had been born in July 1856, so he was only nine months old. I found the family in the South Australian shipping records for assisted migration, which tell us that they signed up to come to Australia and so advertising was involved – the South Australian colonial government ran advertisements in English newspapers to attract people to the colony.

I do not know how long they stayed in South Australia, but in September 1858, Thomas and Mary Ann had another child, a daughter (Martha Ann), and the child was born in Forest Creek, Victoria. Forest Creek was a gold field. It was a gold rush boom town from around 1851. Soon after, its name was changed to Castlemaine, courtesy of the Chief Goldfields Commissioner, who named it after his Irish uncle, Viscount Castlemaine.

Thomas and Mary Ann moved to another gold mining boom town nearby, Chapel Hill, but tragedy struck. In May 1860, Mary Ann was struck with diphtheria and was dead within a week. It was not uncommon for disease to sweep through mining settlements. Conditions were primitive, and the camps were crowded. Fresh water and fresh food were generally unavailable, especially given that gold-panning in the creeks muddied the water.

Remarkably, Thomas and his little sister Martha did not succumb to the disease. But Thomas the Elder was left alone, a long way from his former home in Cornwall, without family support, and with two young children to care for. Mary Ann's death certificate lists the children: "Thomas, 4 years, and Martha Ann, 1 year and 11 months". It was the "1 year and 11 months" that hit me. Martha was so young that her parents were still counting the months of her life, and now her mother was dead.

I don't know how Thomas Martin survived with his young children. It was three years before he remarried. When he did so, he was much further north in Victoria, at Beechworth, which was another gold-mining town. He had moved around, following the gold, I suppose, but I still see that theme of the Martins as mining experts rather than speculators. He came from a long line of miners; he hadn't left work in an office or a factory to "try his luck".

From Castlemaine, which is south of Bendigo, he was now 180 miles north-east, and just a hop, step and jump from Bethanga. I also have to consider that his death certificate says that he also lived in New South Wales at some time in his life, and that doesn't seem to fit into his later life, given his commitment to Bethanga, so perhaps there was also an excursion to a mining area in New South Wales during these years.

Whatever the facts are about his travels (and I have to imagine him travelling with two young children in tow), it was in Beechworth that he married Jane McCartin, who was the daughter of a carrier and who had been born in the County of Armagh, Ireland. They had five children to accompany Thomas and Martha – John William, Paul, Eliza Jane, Mabel, and Thereasa Elvira. I particularly like the name of the last child, because it is very close to the name of my first child, Elvina.

Elvina is an unusual name. I had not come across anyone else bearing the same name until I was at a country market at Alstonville (northern New South Wales coastal fringe) when I was about fifty. A young lady there selling postcards was called Elvina. I had to tell her that I had a daughter of that name and I hadn't come across another Elvina until now. She laughed, and told me her story. Her experience was the same until just a week earlier, when a lady had come up to her and told her that she had the same name. So there are three Elvinas around, and a century earlier, there was an Elvira.

41

While Thomas had come to Australia as a baby, Jane had arrived in Victoria just a few years prior to her marriage to him. Her death certificate says she was born in Ireland and at the time of her death in 1918 she had been living in Victoria for sixty years. I can't be positive about the details of the five children they had between them, because I could not find the birth record for any of them. My understanding is that it was not uncommon for births not to be registered. This was a period of Australian history when the population of a town could go from fifty to five hundred, or even five thousand, in the space of one year, as people flocked to search for gold in new areas.

Comparing the death certificates of Thomas and Jane, I see that the names of the children are not all identical, although there are five of them and the ages are loosely consistent. But Eliza was also Elizabeth, Mabel was also Mary, and middle names have been dispensed with on Jane's death certificate. When she died, at Brunswick North in Melbourne, two of the children were already deceased – John and Eliza.

This is not a trail that I pursue. These children are step-children of one of my great great grandfathers. I have to try not to stray too far. But I include them here because I am sketching the shape of the tree, and Jane and these children were the people who were around when Thomas the Younger was growing up. Perhaps Thomas the Elder met Jane when Thomas the Younger was five or six years old, and their first child was born when young Thomas was about eight.

There was a pause of nine years before another child was born, and then there were three in quick succession, and after that it was seven years before the last child, Theresa, was born. A late baby: Jane was now forty-five, and husband Thomas was forty-nine. By this time, Thomas the Younger was already married in

Bethanga, and he and Phillipa's third child (William Thomas, my grandfather) was born the same year.

In piecing together this part of the story, I realise that Thomas and Jane could have gone to New South Wales after they got married, rather than Thomas travelling alone with the two young children. I had not been able to find the birth records of any of the children in Victoria, but maybe some of them could have been born in New South Wales. And this idea yielded gold (so to speak) – I found both Paul and Eliza, both born in Albury in 1873 and 1874 respectively.

I could not find the birth of John in New South Wales, so I have to assume that Thomas and family stayed in Victoria in the 1860s, perhaps checking out different gold fields as they burst onto the scene. We know that gold was discovered in a significant way at Bethanga in 1876, and it was that event that most likely brought him there. I got a better idea of when that happened by doing another search for the child called, variously, Mabel and Mary, in both New South Wales and Victoria.

I did not find any likely record in Victoria, but I found 'Mary J' born to Thomas and Jane Martin at Albury. It was the date of birth that misled me at first; she was born in 1878, not 1876. So the family was still in Albury in 1878. What were they doing there? And what was the story about the names Mary and Mabel? I am guessing that the two names reflect the same attitude towards that I found in mum's family. You might have an 'official' name that was the one on your birth certificate, but the name by which you were known was different.

My mum is a classic case – Alma Helen on her birth certificate, and Nell in day-to-day life. When she signs her name, or is giving her name and address, she is always Alma Helen, unquestionably. But I don't think it is as simple as this. I think there are other practices at play too. For example, her big sister Frances was always called Frances, and I never heard any other name mentioned in relation to her. But I could not find her birth record until I discovered that her real name was Alice Frances. What was even more telling was this: I told mum what I had found out, and she had no idea that that was her sister's real (official) name.

If we give Jane the last word, because she died fourteen years after Thomas, and her death record is so nicely complete and informative, then her child's name is Mary.

42

There were two other things I noticed on Thomas and Jane's marriage certificate. The first was that she was illiterate. Instead of her signature, there was a cross on the page, and above it the word 'her', and below it the word 'mark'. I have seen this on numerous certificates now, and it has always been written the same way, the cross in the middle, and the 'his or her mark' written above and below it. I saw this on two certificates in quick succession: Thomas and Jane's in 1863 and on Thomas's son's marriage certificate (son Thomas) when he married Phillipa Dower in 1879 at Bethanga.

Seeing the cross was another of those stunning moments. I had got used to seeing marriage certificates with the signatures of the parties. Of course, I knew that universal literacy is a relatively recent phenomenon, but this brought it close to home. Not to know how to read or write was to see your own marriage certificate as an impenetrable code, something to which you were a stranger, and you were asked to pick up a pen and draw two short lines just so, in just that place, see, where they tell you that your own name is written down.

Not to know how to read and write means that everything around you that is written down or printed is alien to you. It means that you have to do your best to avoid any situation where that would place you under threat or cause you to show your ignorance. It means developing a host of strategies to get what you need (food, clothes, anything) – verbally, by establishing standardised routines, by enlisting others to help you, inadvertently as far as possible. It is a fugitive life.

Thomas the Elder could read and write, as could his son. I am sure this happened with the minimal or non-existent involvement of anything so formal as a school. I think that the basis of literacy was functionality. Thomas the Elder was, from the beginning, more than a labourer in the mines; he tended machinery, and he was groomed for management, as we would say. Somehow, in the process, literacy happened.

There was a second thing I had noticed on the marriage certificate. Jane McCartin was Catholic. A closer look reveals that she came from the County of Armagh, part of what is now Northern Ireland, and on those grounds I might have expected her to be Protestant. I found some Irish relatives on mum's side too, who were also from County Armagh (coincidence), and they were buried as Presbyterian (wife) and Church of England (husband). But Jane was indeed Catholic.

After I had followed the history of Thomas Martin in Bethanga, I found a newspaper article about his death, which was a glowing tribute to his contributions to the good fortunes of the gold mine at Bethanga. One sentence that caught my attention, however, was not about his pursuit of his profession, but about his religion: "He was attended in his closing hours by the Very Rev. Father O'Connor, and, fortified by the last rites of the church, passed peacefully away".

Given that he had married an Irish Catholic woman and was married to her for some forty years, it is no surprise that he was afforded the last rites of the Catholic Church on his death bed. However, the abiding religion of the Martin family was Methodism. When son Thomas (or Thomas the Younger) got married in 1879, it was in a Wesleyan ceremony, and when his eldest daughter, Mary Ann, in turn got married, it was according to the rites of the Australian Methodist Church.

I understand the influence of partners. Thomas the Elder got married as a Catholic. He was a widower with two young children marrying a lady who would take care of them. Changing his religion was part of the arrangement, or a consideration, a practical accommodation to what would achieve the best balance in the mix of family members' desires, needs and expectations. Was Jane's adherence to her religion about maintaining her bond with her parents, or was it about maintaining a bond with the home she had left behind in Armagh?

In the same way, how do I understand Thomas the Younger getting married under Wesleyan rites in Bethanga? Was it again about the influence of the partner and her family? The Dowers had come from the same place, Cornwall, indeed, the same part of Cornwall, at Crowan, about twenty miles from St Ives, where Thomas Martin was born. The Dowers (Phillipa's parents) were both buried as Methodists.

But I have another theory about this too. Young Thomas's mother had died when he was four, and his father had only become a Catholic upon marrying Jane. So was young Thomas retrieving a connection with his biological mother by marrying as a Wesleyan Methodist? I don't need to prove this. That is not the point. The point is that this is part of the structure of the situation, and when we make decisions and perform actions, there are many reasons that coexist. And that is where the written records can offer an insight into reality that is intriguing and tantalising.

The reason for my noticing the religious reference in the newspaper article on Thomas Martin's death was because of a story about my own father, Sydney James Martin. He had been married before. We kids knew that, but I didn't know her name. My sister told me it was a big family scandal in dad's family when he got married. It was about religion. She believed that dad's first wife was Jewish, and that was the scandal. We weren't quite sure what denomination the Martin family was, but I had asked mum, and she thought they had been Methodist.

I checked on the death certificate for dad's Uncle Paul, the one that brought him up, and his wife, Maud. It checked out: both of them were buried as Methodists. That was a good indicator; the family was Methodist, and dad in particular had been brought up as a Methodist.

When I found out dad's first wife's name and purchased the marriage certificate, it was full of surprises. No, Olive was not Jewish, but she was Roman Catholic. I guessed that that was the scandal. Dad had turned his back on the family's religion and not only that, he had gone to Rome, overturning five hundred years of church reformation.

I hardly considered my father to be a religious firebrand, but if there was a family furore about dad's marriage, and they subsequently ostracised him, this is the kind of thinking that would usually lie behind it. During my childhood, dad did not go to church at all except for weddings.

If that was the scandal, it is hugely ironic. Dad's own great grandfather married twice, and the second marriage, which lasted over forty years and until his death, was to a

Roman Catholic woman. He was buried with the rites of Roman Catholic Church.

But there were other things about the marriage certificate that captured my attention, and when I got to the bottom of it (although I speak in haste, I still haven't quite got to the bottom of it all), the story was much more disturbing than I could ever have thought.

The marriage certificate showed me that Dad was only twenty-one, and Olive was twenty-four, so was part of the scandal the fact that dad had married at a young age (for a male), and also married a woman older than him? In most of the marriages I had seen among dad's predecessors, the usual age of marriage for males was the mid-twenties. But I think this would have been only a minor quibble; surely it is not the basis on which to ostracise someone.

But there was something else. While dad's 'conjugal status' was 'bachelor', Olive Jane Coates was not a spinster. Her status was 'divorced petitioner'. That was the real surprise to me, for two reasons. She was only twenty-four, and this information indicated that in her short adult life she had been married to a man, had petitioned for divorce from him, met another man and was marrying him. This was life at a blistering pace.

More than that, she was Catholic, and this was 1935, and I couldn't see how it was possible for a young woman to get married twice in the Catholic Church. Divorce was simply not allowed, except in extreme situations, and how was it that she was getting married again in the church, rather than in some private, discreet, modest venue?

Of course, in retrospect, the clues that Olive was Catholic were there to see. After she died, the children went to live with her sister, Aunty Dorrie, and her and Uncle Wally were Catholic. The two children, Jimmy and

Pattie, were brought up Catholic. I suppose that Aunty Dorrie and Olive could have been Protestants, and Dorrie had married Wally and he had been the Catholic, but sometimes it's the obvious that is what is true.

43

What I was looking into was Thomas Martin (the elder) and his life at Bethanga. It is a haphazard business, this looking into things. It is a bit like mining – sometimes you just end up with a disorderly and confusing pile of soil, and sometimes you find great treasures. There is an element of mystery about it too, because things disappear in the mist.

It's as if you are one of those Cornish miners, and you are walking three miles down the road in the early dawn to get to your shift at the mine, and the grass on either side of you is sighing, and the mist is shifting around you and there could be creatures in the mist, who may or may not wish you harm. Or they may simply wish to tell you a tale of utmost sadness or longing. Things move without speaking, the mist has secrets and just occasionally there will be a suggestion, an intimation of things that have been but are now gone. But they are not really gone, they accompany you down the road in silence, and when you get to the mine you start work and you don't have to think about that anymore. Only, when you walk home again, and now it is late in the day, the shadows do what the mist did in the morning, they sweep around you and suggest what cannot quite be seen.

Just so, I found that news article about Thomas Martin's death, and copied it. Now, when I try to go back to the website, it has vanished, like those shapes in the mist. But here I have it; it is from *The Wodonga and Towong Sentinel*, Friday 6th May 1904. It starts: "Deceased was a native of St. Ives, Cornwall, England, and landed at Adelaide in 1857."

There begins a passionate and deferential account of his life and his achievements at Bethanga. The end of Thomas's days is described thus:

> *Mr Martin's health did not improve in Melbourne, so a few weeks ago he decided to come to Chiltern and end his declining years near his relatives. His medical advisers held out no hope of his recovery, as the dread malady had taken too severe a hold upon him, and at his advanced age (seventy years), and his strength and health so much impaired, it was hardly to be expected he would overcome it.*

Upon Thomas's inevitable death, the funeral was held at Chiltern:

> *The funeral cortege on Friday moved from the deceased gentleman's late residence, Chiltern, and was very lengthy, comprising many mourners from Bethanga, Wodonga, and other parts of the district. The service at the grave was impressively read by the Rev. Fathers Ryan (Wodonga) and O'Connor (Chiltern).*

In the account of Thomas Martin's life I learn many things. I learn what he did when he first arrived in Australia. He built a flour mill in Adelaide and operated a successful business there for a few years. This was an unexpected fact, given the tradition of mining from which he sprang.

However, Thomas returned to his mining interests in Victoria, where he met a businessman called J.A. Wallace. Wallace was interested in gold mining as a business, while Thomas had extensive knowledge of how to extract gold from quartz, from his Cornwall past. During the period of time when I thought was living at

Albury (before about 1880), Thomas was actually involved in a number of mines in New South Wales.

The newspaper article mentioned several areas in New South Wales: Barambogie, Golden Bay, Hawksview and Yarrara. These are within reach of Albury. I found another news article from 1894 which talks about Hawksview. A prospector had found gold, but the history of the area was that despite some rich patches, there were no continuous reefs that could be reliably mined for a profit. The article says: "Some time ago Hawksview was worked by several Albury syndicates, but the claims were eventually abandoned as being unprofitable and owing to the royalty levied by the owner." (*Bathurst Free Press and Mining Journal*, 21 May 1894)

I suspect that Thomas Martin and Mr Wallace were involved. The article included a story that gives you some idea of the rich possibilities that hovered about: "Several phenomenally rich lodes and leads were struck here (Hawksview), as much as £190 worth of gold being obtained from one bucket of dirt." One tends to forget this in the midst of all the tales of disappointment and hardship on the goldfields. So I think: never forget the dream that drives people onwards.

Yet I still say that the drivers for Martin and Wallace were different. Their goal was sustainable yield, an ongoing business, not a quick hit that would allow them to live the rest of their lives as idle gentlemen and ladies. Wallace was an entrepreneur who later became a Member of the Victorian Parliament.

After that reef of gold, along with copper, was discovered on New Year's Day in 1876, J.A. Wallace soon set up a company to establish a deep-shaft mine and extraction plant, and Thomas Martin became the mine manager. The difficulty the company faced was that although the gold and copper were present, their process for extracting the minerals from the quartz was not working efficiently enough. Advice was sought from mining engineers around the world: France, Germany, America and Great Britain.

Despite all the advice and suggestions, and the expenditure of many thousands of pounds on experiments and equipment, the problem had not been solved, and it looked as if the company would have to close the mine, which had not yet returned a dividend to the shareholders. Some of the attempts also set the townspeople against the mine, because they involved burning the ore for a month in open heaps, generating choking fumes that blanketed the town.

A recent account by the Federal Department of the Environment, which was looking at the historical significance of the mining site and processing plant, describes what happened next: "Having spent more than 10 years trawling the globe for experts to (find a viable extraction process), Wallace's problem was finally solved by his own works manager". The account says that Thomas Martin knew the Bethanga ore better than anybody. He focused on one of the older processes, but made a number of modifications to it, and the furnaces were rebuilt as well. ("Wallace Smelting Works, Martins Road, Bethanga, Victoria"; www.environment.gov.au)

The revised process was successful, and the Bethanga mine became profitable, both for copper and for gold. By 1895, the Wallace Bethanga Company had attracted a takeover bid, and Bethanga Goldfields Limited was formed, with Thomas Martin being appointed the first chairman of directors. He held this position for almost ten years, until his failing health forced him to relinquish the position.

The article on Thomas Martin's death in 1904 says that he was known as "the father of Bethanga" for his role in establishing the Bethanga gold fields. Thomas often said that solving the problem of extracting the ore, and establishing a viable mine, was the dream of his life. As well as being noted on the Department of Environment's heritage listing, Thomas Martin's innovations are discussed in a PhD thesis, "The Development of Mining Technology in Australia, 1801 – 1945", by Ralph Winter Birrell (The University of Melbourne, 2005).

But it was not just his engineering prowess for which he was respected. He was also seen as an outstanding manager, one who cared for the people around him. To quote the article again: "Frequently, in the absence of a medical man, was he called out to set a broken limb or advise in the case of an illness, and many a one has occasion to remember, with gratitude, his kindnesses in these and other directions."

He was buried at Chiltern, where he lived towards the end of his life. I have not been there, but I have a photograph taken of the headstone on his grave. There are people who travel around cemeteries and take pictures of headstones and post them on a website, indexed by name. It was in this way that I came by the image of the headstone (and I am grateful). I think it is amazing. This is what it says:

> *By the Employees of the Bethanga Goldfields Co Ltd. To the memory of Thomas Martin, their late manager who laboured among them for 25 years and earned the respect and goodwill of all. Born at St Ives, Cornwall, England. Died aged 70 years. We loved him.*

I have never read anything like this on a headstone. It is a message from a whole community, far beyond family, and it is a message of utmost respect. Those last three words: "We loved him". I think of the world I live in, just more than one hundred years later, and I try to imagine a group of employees formulating a message to go on the headstone of their recently deceased manager's grave. It is difficult to think of any manager about whom the words, "We loved him" would spring to mind.

Yet what Thomas Martin did, and the person that he was, do not seem beyond the reach of ordinary people. He was smart, to be sure, and determined, and he respected and cared for those who worked for him. None of this is superhuman. But then, I think, he did this for a lifetime; it was not a charade. It was an admirable life.

44

I wonder if my father had any knowledge of this history. If he did not hear about it from his own father, because the family was split up when he was small, then perhaps he heard about it from his Uncle Paul while growing up. And where did that leave him? Did he grow up with a feeling that the glory days were behind them, that his and the family's future was a mediocre existence in the anonymous, interminable streets of the inner suburbs of a city, serving out time in a nondescript job?

I think of my father going away from the city to work on that farm on the Hawkesbury River. Did he want to get out of the city? There were some of the family who didn't come to Sydney around the turn of the century; they stayed in the Bethanga area, and some become farmers. One of the stories mum told me was that after she and dad were married, and before they settled at Greenacre, they had discussed leaving Sydney and finding a position on a farm as a couple, helping out with the farm work. It didn't happen.

My memory of growing up in Greenacre was of a growing sense of claustrophobia as all the bush was cleared and houses were built to fill up the streets. When the whole street was done, the developers then cut roads into the middle of all the blocks, forced the subdivision of all the existing blocks of land, and filled up the middle with more houses. When I was twenty-four, I got out of Sydney, and I didn't come back until I was in my late forties.

Somehow, now I think it can't hurt me. But I am very glad that I did get out as a young man. And now I wonder whether any of this thinking came from my father. I never got the impression that he was overjoyed with his life, and a lot of that was not about our family, it was situational – the environment, the work, the mundane necessity of it all.

45

It strikes me that this wonderful story about Thomas Martin (the Elder) is what many family histories aim towards, and having reached it, you feel, it is all done. There are television shows where celebrities explore their past and find unexpected things. But the trajectory of these shows always seems to be towards one person, who is the key to understanding the whole family, and often, as a bonus, this found ancestor is the key to our well-known celebrity having a deeper understanding of him/herself.

I think that my Thomas Martin is a very powerful figure in my family's history. I think his impact on the Martin side of the family has been immense. The story of a life like that makes a deep impression on children and on siblings and on people further out in the family constellation. Then the deeper psychic strands of that story's meaning seep into the bones of everyone who is related. It becomes the job of each of us to be aware of the feelings that stir us, even if we have no idea where they come from. Like feeling claustrophobic in a circumstance where most people think they are being ushered into the land of promise. It is our stance towards those feelings, whether it is blind following, acceptance or re-appraisal, that determines what we make of ourselves. We have that choice: innovate or replicate.

Thomas Martin is important, but there are others, across both mum's and dad's sides of the family. I want to map out more of this territory, because there are questions to be asked about that wider terrain. Even to answer questions that are simple, like, when did all my ancestors come to Australia? And, were any of my ancestors convicts?

There are more stories of mum's that I have to find the facts for as well. "The Archer family owned a hotel at Pyrmont called the Duke of Edinburgh. It had a white horse."

And there is more to be said about my dad's first marriage, and the lady he married.

[Additional information: As noted earlier, while finalising this book I had contact from a relative on the Martin side of the family, Nola Nixon, and she knew a lot more about the lives of the Martin family in Bethanga. The information I received from her confirms what I have written above, but she also knew of further sources. For example, Thomas Martin, manager of the Wallace Bethanga mining company, has been written about in a book called *A poor man's diggings*, by June Philipp.

Considering the book's title, I can see how that thinking is part of our family's ethos that has come down through the generations – hard work and modest expectations. And this is a good place to end this book. I started out knowing nothing but a few stories, and now I can talk about "our family".]

Family trees

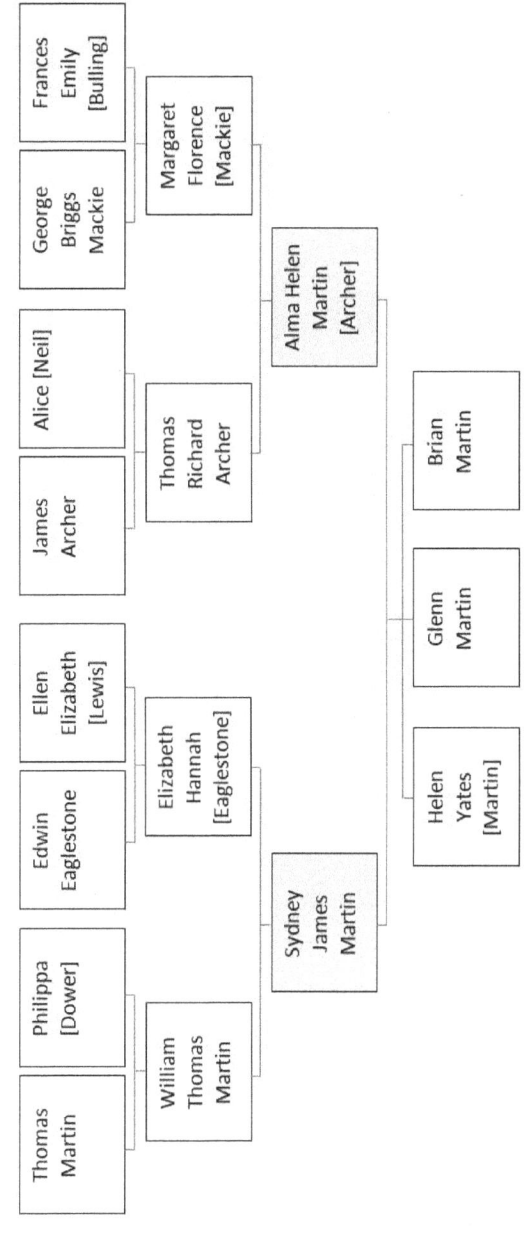

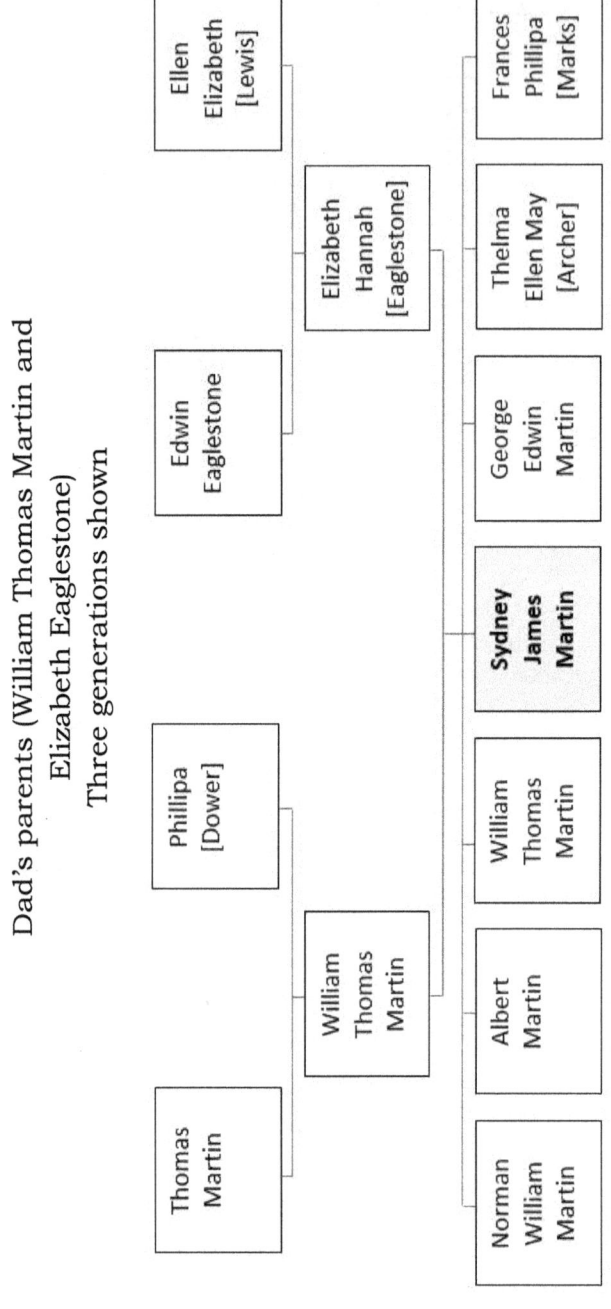

Dad's parents (William Thomas Martin and Elizabeth Eaglestone)
Three generations shown

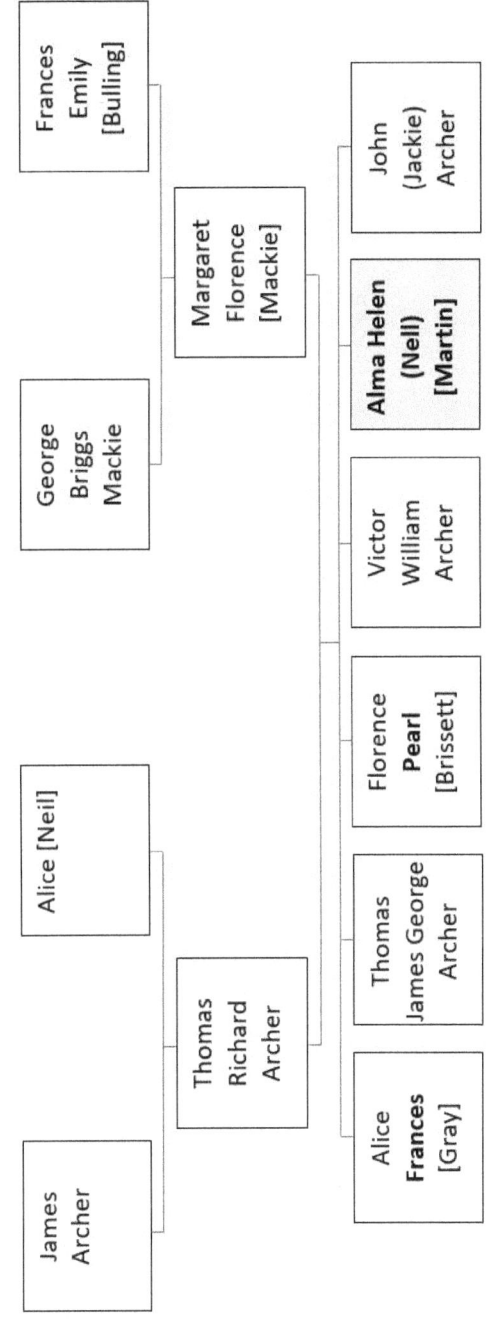

Mum's parents (Thomas Richard Archer and Margaret Florence Mackie)
Three generations shown

www.ingramcontent.com/pod-product-compliance
Lightning Source LLC
Chambersburg PA
CBHW031957080426
42735CB00007B/428